CHEAT MODE

The definitive guide to getting into and surviving the games industry

By

Dan Jacobs

Thanks to everyone who helped out on this project

Special thanks to Blitz Games and Women in Games for all their help

Eurogamer.net and Gamesindustry.biz for all their support

Vanessa Matte for the beautiful cover art

Every single person taking the time out to be interviewed, you are all amazing

And James Grant for keeping me employed

Contents

Insert Coin

At the end of the 90's I found myself with few qualifications, between jobs and without a clue what to do with my life. Out of the blue I got a call from a good friend I had worked with in the past. We had helped each other to find work and now she was working as a secretary for a local games developer who needed testers to help out with their Christmas releases and she asked whether I was interested. I think I almost fell over considering the possibilities of playing games for a living, but there was one problem, I had never done anything like it in my life. My friend explained how she had spoken to one of the testers and all he had done was apply with a list of games he had completed to show his interest in video games. She suggested that I should do the same, so I did. One nerve racking interview later and I walked into a games developer for my first day at work. A decade later and I found myself in another games developer, only this time I was a Q.A. manager about to meet my own team and begin helping them along the path to their own careers in videogames. To this day I'm unsure as to which was the scarier prospect.

In between the two companies, I had filled my resume with several world renowned companies and several less successful ones. Some are still going today and others have sadly departed, but every single one had something to teach me about the industry and it's that knowledge that I want to share in this book. My route into the industry was pretty much down to luck, but to continue to thrive and build a career in the industry has always been down to me. To do so I've worked long and hard to be an asset on every project I've worked on. I've sacrificed my free time and relationships to make my career the career I wanted. I've spent three days and two nights at my desk. I've commuted for 2 hours each way everyday to get to work and I've travelled the country from Edinburgh to Brighton. I've visited Canada and Germany and met a whole host of interesting folk just trying to create a videogame people will enjoy. It's these experiences I want to share with you, I want to help you get into the industry I love, I want you to enter it knowing what to expect and I want to see it filled with passionate people who share their worlds, their stories, their characters with the next generation of gamers. In this book we'll look at how the industry works, what career possibilities there are and how you can make it into those careers. We'll speak to industry professionals from all sorts of positions to find out how they got where they are today. We'll even speak to those people not directly involved in actually making the game, but without whom we couldn't make the games you love and enjoy. As well as exploring all of this we'll be looking at the working life in the games industry and what you can expect.

If you want to work in games, if you want to create and share, engage and entertain, if you want to be a part of the latest games millions around the world enjoy, then this guide will help you get on the path to your own career in videogames.

Throughout this book you'll find speech bubbles just like this one. These comments are from real industry professional, many of whom have worked in the games industry for years. These comments are here to help you understand what working in the industry is really like. Please note these comments are the views of the interviewees and not the companies they work for.

Chapter 1: Multiplayer

Let's start by looking at the way the industry works and how a game goes from initial concept to a product on the shelf. We'll also look at the complex relationship between a publisher and a developer, how they work together and what each company gets from this relationship. With this knowledge you'll begin to see how the industry works and which company would give you the best start in your career.

To begin with we should understand the two main parties involved, a developer, the people who make the game and a publisher, the people who publish the game. This is easily compared to the music industry where we have the artist (developers) and the record companies (publishers). Publishers often have development teams or even development companies working for them in addition to working with external developers. Traditionally the two companies need each other to make a game and each provides support for the other, the chart below shows how both companies benefit from this partnership.

Publisher Provides
Financial Backing
Equipment
Staff Resources
Manufacture the game
Distribution
Marketing

Developer Gains
Money to finance the project
Equipment to make and test the game
Extra staff if necessary
Game made into a sellable package
Distribution
Marketing for the game

Developer Provides
A unique game
Unique set of tools and tech
Specialised service

Publisher Gains
A unique title for their library
Tech in their game which others cannot provide
A specialist in that product type

A developer usually provides a specialised service which the publisher couldn't obtain elsewhere. This could be anything from converting a game from one platform to another, to expertise in certain tools, tech or platforms. Whatever specialist services a developer offers it will probably be something unique that the publisher needs. When we look at the charts above, it's easy to think that the publisher loses out in the arrangement, but they tend to earn a bigger percentage of the profits for their part of the deal. It's also very important not to underestimate the value of a unique game. If the developer in question creates a triple A game then the profits can be phenomenal (Triple A games are highly successful products which sell well worldwide and gain high review scores). Additionally, since they provide the finance for the game, the publisher has the final say. Even if what they require is harmful to the title it will be done.

For an example of this complex and occasionally painful relationship, let's go back to when I was working on a game with a peripheral. The publisher wanted a calibration screen to calibrate the additional peripheral and we explained how it didn't need one. Arguments like "the calibration is fine"; "nothing will be gained from this" and "we have little time left to complete the work" all fell on deaf ears and of course because the publisher calls the shots a calibration screen was added. The game shipped with a screen which calibrated nothing at all, everyone was happy and the customer was none the wiser. So just like any relationship in life we can see that this one can be challenging at times. However challenging, both teams need each other to create a successful game. In the scenario below we'll look at the most common way a game is made and how these two companies work together.

Both publishers and developers have positives, for example working at a publisher will get you a lot of varied experience very quickly due to the fact that they generally have a lot more product passing through their doors whereas working for a developer you'll have a lot more input into the game.

-Paul Sedgmore
Q.A. Manager, Colossal Games

So we know that the two companies work together to make a game, but how is this done? To answer this we should look at a typical scenario for making a console game.

The developer I work for has had a great idea for a new game. It has been discussed and we've decided that this is a project we'd like to pursue. So a few select people are removed from an on-going project and given the task of taking the initial idea and turning it into a pitch document. This document will be used in meetings with perspective publishers in the hope that they will get excited and become interested in the potential game, with the end goal being a game being signed to a publisher so that the actual work can begin. A pitch document can take many forms, anything from a playable demo, a video or just a document outlining the game's unique selling points (USP's). It's important to remember that the games' industry is a business and no matter how good an idea is, if the developers don't get across how this will make money for the publisher the pitch will probably fail.

After several meetings and much discussion the team will have decided to create a demo of the product and back this up with high quality concept art work. At this point the developer starts speaking to perspective publishers and arranges some meetings and eventually they have success. A publisher loves the pitch and the legal work begins to sign the game to the publisher. The contract that they create will be (in essence) the game's birthing plan, as it covers the legal responsibilities of each party and what they'll do to give life to the title. Included in the document is the budget for every aspect of the game's creation, from marketing to development and distribution. Importantly it will contain the key dates involved in the development of the title. The parties barter, haggle and work out a contract they're happy with before both sign the documentation and work can actually begin. A small team is needed to start production and usually you'll need a producer, a designer, a good sized code team (at least three or four) and some artists and animators. These team members work together to get the title ready for the first milestone (team size will of course vary from company to company, but this example will give you some idea of how big each team is throughout the development process).

The publisher will aid the developer in production with any resources it can spare so quite often teams will be formed from both companies:

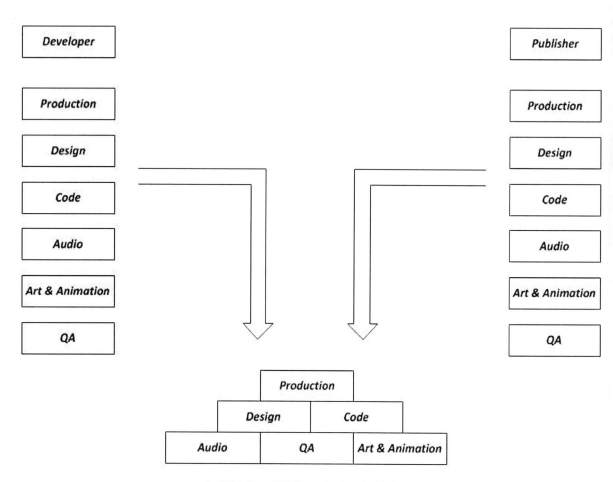

The Actual Team Who Create The Game

While the team busy themselves for the first milestone, let's look at what a milestone is (we'll explore each department and their roles in making a game later in this book). Milestones are specific dates when the game is presented to the publisher. These presentations are very important because of the way a game is funded. A developer gets funding from the publisher to create the game, this money is essential to pay the staff and keep production moving. A publisher wants to fund production, but also ensure a high level of quality true to the pitch and concept work they've been shown as a game takes a long time to develop and is very expensive to make. These dates are set out at the start and each individual milestone is given specific criteria which have to meet the publisher's approval. Once approval has been gained the developer is paid for that part of the production and work continues.

their games, made money and naturally expanded. Although it never died out, it had become almost extinct until recent technological advances, higher internet speeds and reliability improvements coupled with the take off of smart phones, the ease of access to information and the huge interest in social networking created a rebirth of the early days of games with the market exploding as smaller developers hoping to make their money in the smart phone or social networking arena have easily and quickly setup their own companies. I've lost count of the amount of start up companies in the last few years hoping to jump into this lucrative and exciting market. The reason so many companies are joining this new wave is due to the simplicity of creating games for this market. They tend to be one screen titles with simple (if any) story line and little audio or video required which massively reduces the time, money and staff need to take a game from concept to sales, with of course complete freedom over what they make and how. It removes the need for a publisher and allows a company to produce many more titles over the course of a year. Due to this recent expansion we've seen a massive change in the industry. New companies, new platforms and a direct way of getting to the consumer have all combined to give us an exciting area of development where people can develop their ideas more quickly and easily than ever before. With new customer bases that didn't exist five years ago, companies are falling over themselves to catch up and enter this market with established publishers like Disney and EA entering the space. It's important to point out that this could really work for you and your career and if it's not what you want to do, don't dismiss it but try to remember that opportunities for work and work experience programmes are positive things and that all experience is good and can only enhance your resume as you try to get into traditional games development.

Chapter 2: The Quest Begins

Now we know how a game is created, we can begin to focus on getting the role we want and our first application to perspective companies. The most important thing about your application is to stand out from the crowd. Hundreds of people apply to junior roles daily and the only way you're going to get that all important interview is to convey your passion and drive for the industry. When I last opened a role for a new tester to join our team, I had 60 applicants to check through without advertising the role. This is a highly competitive industry and as such you need to do everything you can to stay ahead of the crowd. As mentioned in the introduction all I ever did was simply include a list of games I had completed and ensured my covering letter spoke about my passion and drive. You have to remember this was before the internet had really taken off so competition, although still high, was nowhere near the levels it is today. So what can someone starting out today do to improve their chances? To begin with let's look at a couple of well known examples of people pushing creativity to improve their chances at working in the industry. When Tim Schafer of Monkey Island fame landed his first job at Lucasarts he felt that he had blown the phone interview section and as such had nothing to lose so he sent in his covering letter in the form of a text based adventure game.

Your quest for the ideal career begins, logically enough, at the Ideal Career Center. Upon entering, you see a helpful looking woman sitting behind a desk. She smiles and says, "May I help you?"

>SAY YES I NEED A JOB

"Ah," she replies, "and where would you like to work, Los Angeles, Silicon Valley, or San Rafael?"

>SAY SAN RAFAEL

"Good choice," she says, "Here are some jobs you might be interested in," and gives you three brochures.

>EXAMINE BROCHURES

The titles of the three brochures are as follows: "HAL Computers: We've Got a Number For You," "Yoyodine Defense Technologies: Help Us Reach Our Destructive Potential," and "Lucasfilm, Ltd: Games, Games, Games!"

>OPEN LUCASFILM BROCHURE

The brochure says that Lucasfilm is looking for an imaginative, good-humored team player who has excellent communication skills, programming experience, and loves games. Under that description, oddly enough, is a picture of you.

>SEND RESUME

You get the job! Congratulations! You start right away!

>GO TO WORK

You drive the short commute to the Lucasfilm building and find it full of friendly people who show you the way to your desk.

>EXAMINE DESK

Your desk has on it a powerful computer, a telephone, some personal nicknacks, and some work to do.

>EXAMINE WORK

It is challenging and personally fulfilling to perform.

>DO WORK

As you become personally fulfilled, your score reaches 100, and this quest comes to an end. The adventure, however, is just beginning and so are your days at Lucasfilm.

THE END

This highly unusual and creative method would clearly stand out from any normal covering letter and most importantly demonstrates passion, drive and enthusiasm. You can read the full story from the man himself at:
http://www.doublefine.com/news/comments/twenty_years_only_a_few_tears/

In a case of history repeating itself, an applicant recently made the news by applying to Double Fine in exactly the same way. You can actually play his game/application at:

all it must work. If you're showing off your code skills and the employer needs to debug it to get it to run then it speaks volumes about your abilities or apparent lack of them, no matter how advanced that code might be. If your animations on display are missing frames or have poorly chosen camera angels then this reflects badly on your skills. No matter what, the show reel must contain finished work. Remember that employers see a lot of show reels so try to ensure yours is the one that catches their attention, make it easy to browse, use common sense on what you present and how you present it and above all don't let yourself down by showing half finished or old work. An up to date show reel can only increase your chances of getting that all important interview. If you need some help designing and maintaining your show reel check out the resources section where you can find some helpful hints and tips from professionals.

> *A show reel is all you have when it comes down to it. This is the thing that shows your practical skills off, a polished reel (or level, or game) goes to elevate you above everyone else vying for your job. You have to remember you're not only trying to prove yourself capable and employable, you're competing with a ton of other people who you have to assume have very similar skill-sets. So then it comes down to how you present those skills that counts.*
>
> *-Andrew Smith*
> *Designer & Founder, Split Milk Studios*

Work Experience

Want to enhance your prospects even further? A work experience programme may be just the right thing for you and many studios offer work experience to people aged sixteen and upwards. Use the studio map in the resource section to find your local studios, write to them and see if they need a hand with anything. It might be the ideal way to get your foot in the door, enhance your resume and it will help you to get started networking with industry professionals. You may well be required to attend an interview for a work experience programme, you'll certainly need to before starting a job. If you do secure an interview it's tempting to get carried away, so remember an interview is still a step away from actual employment. Now let's look at what a games industry interview might consist of and how we can improve our chances of turning an interview into gainful employment.

> *I organized work experience at Kuju Surrey where I met my future Art Director at Doublesix. I went on to do another unpaid work placement just as Doublesix formed. Those placements allowed me to make an impression on some artists who would later be in a position to hire me. Of course for an artist it's all about a high quality and relevant portfolio though.*
>
> *-Daniel Lodge*
> *Lead Artist, Doublesix Games*

The N.D.A.

Before any interview in the industry begins or when you start work for the first day you will be required to sign an N.D.A. or Non Disclosure Agreement. This is a legally binding document between yourself and the studio/publisher which basically says that you agree not to talk about any projects you see, the project you work on or others that may be in development at the company. This means you should not discuss it with anyone, friends, family, etc. The games company (your employer) has to release info. About their game as and when they're ready to and it can be very harmful if any unique features of the game enter the public domain early. I've worked for companies which actually have teams of people trawling the net for mentions of their games which may break the N.D.A. One colleague of mine lost his job because he had mentioned on a forum that the sequel wasn't as good as the original game. He used his gamer-tag as his forum ID, was traced and no longer works there. So learn from his mistakes, take the N.D.A. for what it is (a legally binding document) and play it safe. The only way to ensure you don't break it is to not discuss your project until it's released. You are of course allowed to discuss a title once it has been released, but even then I would be wary of discussing any of the production methods.

The interview itself

No matter what else the interview process contains, we can say for certain that will contain an interview with the department manager, lead or both. They will ask you questions just like a real job interview to see if you would fit well with the existing team and project, whether you have the aptitude and skill sets. Be prepared for some unusual questions. A friend of mine was asked his favourite doughnut type was and I've frequently been asked about my gaming systems and habits. Below we have some questions you're likely to be asked in a games interview.

Why do you want to work for this company?

This question in one form or another is almost certainly going to come up so, make sure you've researched the company, their past successes and failures and what the project might be. Highlight any games of theirs you might have loved and explain why that makes you want to be part of their team.

What is your favourite type of game?

Our first gaming question, this could be a ploy to ascertain if you like the upcoming game they could be working on. Either way, you know your favourites and your dislikes so be honest and passionate and you'll be fine.

> *Attend shows and events. BAFTA and the Eurogamer Expo are just two that do a hell of a lot to present keen folk with the chance to talk to developers. This is a tactic that can work. An example: There's a guy who came to hear me talk at the EG Expo two years running. He'd never worked in games, he was just finishing university on the second occasion, but I've now tried to hire him three times. I'll get him one day, but the point is, he was a clear talent, had something to say - and show - for himself, he's already a success.*
>
> *-Jez Harris*
> *Production Manager, Supermassive Games*

Have you got any experience of the submission process?

We've discussed the submission process in detail earlier, it may also be called standards. No matter if you haven't got direct experience, explain this but also use the opportunity to tell them what the process is and why it's important in games development. This shows you have gone out of your way to learn about the industry prior to attempting to join it.

Can you name some common submission issues?

O.K. we get the general idea of submission, but what are these standards and what do they cover? Sadly I'm not allowed to print a copy of the standards used during the submission process, but in essence they cover a lot and vary from each console. However I can tell you they whatever company it is, they have standards for networking, saving, peripherals, trophies or achievements, ejecting the disk and controllers.

Have you any experience with bug databases?

Whatever department you applied to they will be using the Q.A. bug database, although they are all very similar there are some differences between each database. We take a look at the Q.A. process later on in this book so even if you have no direct experience you can at least explain what they are and how they are used.

Have you ever been involved in focus or Beta testing?

Focus testing happens for many different products. It's when the target audience is invited to check the product out before launch and give their thoughts. Beta testing is when the public are invited in to help test the software. This is primarily to test the servers to check that they can handle the online traffic, but in recent times it is also becoming a promotional tool. If you have been involved in either of these then brilliant, explain what product, when you did it and how you found it. If not then, just like before, explain what they are (I would highly recommend partaking in a Beta programme before any industry interviews).

What stages of production have you been involved with? (Pre-Alpha, Alpha, Beta)

We've discussed the important milestones earlier on and if you've done a Beta test you're aware of what a game is like by that stage. So if you have no familiarity at least talk about your awareness of them. This question is unlikely to come up unless you have some experience, if you get the chance to ask any questions it might be worth asking what stage of development they're at for the project.

> *Don't be disheartened by any rejection letters you get; ask for feedback if possible and adapt. Keep applying to as many studios/publishers as you can; every reply, interview, rejection letter is experience to build upon. Take part in beta tests to get a feel of what it's like to play unpolished games. Be prepared to move/travel for your dream job.*
>
> *-Nick Scurr*
> *Senior Tester, FreeStyleGames*

What consoles do you currently own?

Another question about your gaming habits, no matter how many consoles you own this a great chance to talk about the market and the distinct appeals of each console on the market.

What's your favourite genre?

Another easy question about your own gaming habits, just answer honestly and it should be no problem. Be aware that this could be a trick question as the potential employers may want to find out if you have an interest in the game they're currently creating. This is just another reason why it's a good idea to researching the company prior to the interview.

Have you experienced any problems with online titles?

Online titles or titles with online elements are very popular. Employers are likely to be working on at least some online features for their title. This adds a lot of complexity to game design, code and test so any experience could be an asset, so it is likely that this question will come up in one form or another.

Have you any experience of the following:

- Training Staff
- Holding meetings/presentations
- Creating documents
- Working without supervision

Experience in these fields can be gained in any industry, so if you are asked about any of the above it's probably a small developer which may be looking for people to take on extra responsibilities. From the above questions we can also deduce that it's likely to be a small team and quite possibly hold the potential to move on and up quickly in the firm. I wouldn't worry about the experience questions since you either have the experience or you don't, the important thing is to show a willingness to learn. No matter what, be calm and think carefully about the questions you get before answering. The good thing about industry interviews is no matter what you get asked they will always have an interest in your gaming and your interest in the industry, so don't be afraid of demonstrating just how passionate you are and how this will be an asset to them.

All of this info is all very well and good, but where do you look for jobs to actually apply for? Towards the end of this book you can find several helpful resources to finding work, ranging from websites to recruitment agencies and the studios themselves. But why limit your chances? Everyone in the development community is out and about just like you, they go to the same events you do and are on the same websites. You have to network to get on, the industry is incredibly small and everyone knows each other. So go out meet these people, talk to them about what they do, what you'd like to do and how you might be able to help.

There's loads of game companies, there's loads of publishes that do little events that are just about sampling games, put on a night in a pub somewhere, just invite loads of people. I'm really amazed because we advertise them sometimes on our forum and I'm really amazed that more people don't go along to little events like that because there will be P.R. and marketing people there that you can talk to.

-Tom Champion
Community Manager, Eurogamer.net

Chapter 3: Pause

We've covered a lot so far, so before we continue let's take a moment to pause, reflect on what we've covered thus far and speak to some developers about their working life. Founded in the '80s by Philip and Andrew Oliver, Blitz Games Studios is one of the U.K.'s oldest and most respected development studios. Currently running six distinct divisions, the company has come a long way from its humble bedroom coding beginnings. In late September 2011, I visited some of the team in their Leamington Spa offices to discuss how they got into the industry and what working on games is really like. Those kindly taking time out from making games to answer my questions were:

- Kim Blake: Senior Events & Education Co-ordinator, 18 years service, 5 years at Blitz
- Becky Hewitt: Junior Designer, 5 years service, 2 years at Blitz
- Darren Watford: Concept Artist, Visualiser, 5 years in the industry at Blitz
- Simon Ible: Senior Character Artist, 11years service, 4 years at Blitz
- Jonathan Tainsh: Design Manager, 13 years service, 10 years at Blitz
- Andrew Shenton: Technical Manager, 12 years service, 4 years at Blitz

Thanks to agreeing to the interview. We're going to start off by looking at your career and what led you into the roles you are in. Why did you want to get into the games industry?

KIM

"I never wanted to get into games. I hated games. I was going out with a game's programmer, a proper bedroom coder and one of his games needed some dialogue written and his producer said: "Well don't you know anyone who can write" and he went "Well yeah my girlfriend can". So I did that, ended up overseeing the voices recording and then putting the wav files into the code. Still didn't enjoy playing games. I can remember saying: "Come back when you can do curves!", but I discovered that the process of making games is absolutely fascinating. It's hard and it's complicated and that meant you got to work with some very creative and intelligent people, solving things that up until yesterday nobody had known needed to be solved and that's why I'm still in games"

BECKY

"Well I'm a bit of an anomaly. I was a scientist before coming to work in the games industry"

"A scientist, in what field?"

"Biology. I worked in a few labs and was totally frustrated and really bored with that industry and my friend suggested that as I like computer games (I'd been playing them since I was about 7 or 8 years old) and I like challenges why didn't I try and get in the games industry. So I literally sent round dozens of emails, to all the games companies I could think of and I got accepted at Evolution Studios as a Q.A. tester and worked there for 3 years before coming to Blitz because it looked really fun"

DARREN

"I was one of these kids that were good at art at school and as an artist (when I was growing up) you were either a book illustrator, a magazine illustrator or, if you were doing concept, it was for films. I really only became aware that video games are (especially as a 2D artist, not a combination 2D/3D artist) a viable option career option ten years ago"

"What made you become aware of it?"

"One of the guys I went to college with ending up working for Criterion where he was doing concept art. I was working in a call centre at the time and I had done nothing with my art. I had always played games and been a gamer primarily since the Commodore 64, Spectrum era. It was kind of like: "Oh wow, if he's doing that then why can't I?" because most games for me are better subject matter, they're like monsters and sci-fi and stuff. So for me I think, unlike a lot of concept artists, I thought that games would be a better subject matter. So basically I went back to college to do a games art course and then I just started sending my C.V. out everywhere. So primarily as a games player it was realising there was an opportunity out there for a 2D artist"

SIMON

"I didn't originally think of going into games. I did visual communications, majoring in illustration and then I started doing graphic design jobs. I was a bit frustrated with the jobs that I was doing, so I went back and did a M.A. in Arts and Design and I was going to go into creating CD-ROMS as this was about 11 or 12 years ago as that was kind of the thing at the time. Then one day at university I saw a tiny little sticker on one of the doors talking about computer games and I love computer games. I stood there thinking "Oh yeah, I didn't think of that". I used to play on the Commodore 64 and that kind of stuff, but I had never been a huge gamer. So I took my portfolio in and applied, got into a position and started building environments, doing concept work and eventually I was encouraged to do lots of little bits of everything that was going on in the studio, which was the nice thing about it. When I was going to go into doing the CD-ROMS I had been initially planning on going to do children's books, but what I liked about this was that you've not got just the imagery, you've also got the sounds and you can get totally immersed in it. Then, thinking about video games, I realised was exactly the same thing, you could get totally immersed, sound and vision. That's why I thought it'd be a really good thing to do/get into"

JONATHAN

"I was always massively creative at school, always doodling rather than working, always thinking of stuff to do, always playing games in my head. I had an Acorn Electron so I used to write games. Well mostly it was just flashing text, if I'm honest"

BECKY

"Was it a rude word?"

JONATHAN

"Yep, nothing's changed. So I went through education, left school without going to university and got a really tedious boring job. I thought I can't do this anymore (I was working for a pensions company, which was the worst thing ever). I did two years of that and then decided to go back to university to do something creative. I did an Art degree in CD-ROMS as well as actually playing a lot of computer games at the time.

The first I ever played was on my dad's till actually, a massive till and a tiny little screen. You could just play well like Space Invaders on it. So I decided I'm going to be creative, went to art college, played a lot of computer games and decided I can make computer games better than anyone else could". Told all my friends I was going to become a games designer, they didn't believe me. I was just like: "You wait till I finish university". I applied for every job under the sun and I had rejection letters all over my bedroom wall literally! I got a job at Codemasters, went up to Q.A. Manager, then swapped it all around and said "Right I'm in now, you can't get rid of me" and became a designer, so I've achieved my goal"

ANDREW

"Both my parents are creative artists, highly respected in their fields. My dad ended up being a teacher. When I was four he got an Acorn Electron, started working out how the logo was done on the screen and then he started involving me in it. I remember being fascinated that my dad could draw on the screen. I was also playing Elite, playing in the loosest sense of the word, kind of just watching it crash. Of course, being a four year old I was stabbing, stabbing lots of buttons, but I was fascinated by the process of making something happen on the screen and that kind of stuck with me. As I grew up I was always playing games. I remember wanting to be involved with games in some way. I remember originally I was confused, I think I wanted to be an artist and I made quite a lot of video game art. What I found was my art would sit there on the screen and nothing would happen and I was like: "Well, when is someone going to come along, wave the magic wand to make things happen and make this into a game" Of course, they didn't. Everything I created was kind of lifeless and just sat there, it didn't do anything. So I took it upon myself to kind of make it work. In doing that I very quickly found that it was incredibly hard and with that, much to my astonishment (as Kim said), that it involved a lot of people. I remember being about 13 I think and being in the bottom set for mathematics, being terrible at maths and being regarded at school as possibly the worst mathematician in the world. Then I realised that to make things move up and down I needed to understand how simultaneous linear equations would work and within three months I was in the top set for maths in the school and I had figured out exactly how this stuff worked. I then had to make what was a rather disgusting choice for me, which meant that around the time 3D graphics came out I was playing around with art, still making games and I had to choose between a technical path to carry on with mathematics and computer games or to carry on doing drawings. I chose maths, further maths, physics and computer games programming as my A levels. I went on and did a M.A. in Computer Science with Artificial Intelligence. I spent two years doing programming which was easy by that point and then I spent a year doing science trying to reproduce parts of the brain and that sort of thing. I got a bit distracted there and I thought my future lay in being a scientist. Then I started getting lots of offers from military companies who wanted me to kind of target missiles for them and analyse for them whether countries were being invaded and that sort of thing. Whilst still playing games I was nearer and nearer to that point of having to make a choice. Seemed apparent to me that a nicer thing to be doing with my time (rather than blowing people up or going missing when I got my code wrong) was actually to have my code crash in people's bedroom. So I didn't kind of fall into it at all. From the age of twelve I knew exactly what I wanted to be doing and I did everything I could, watching TV programmes, going round talking to people. I actually stalked a couple of people who are here now about twelve years ago when they worked at Gremlin in Sheffield. I used to go up and knock on the door and say I'm twelve now can you let me in? They wouldn't have me as a Q.A. tester, but eventually when I qualified for my degree they desperately wanted me as a games programmer. It was interesting because fundamentally the science is the same as working on kind of cutting edge military defence systems. They're not different things it's just kind of the applications that differ"

"So just out of curiosity do you ever regret that kind of crossroads moment where you chose tech over art?"

ANDREW

"Absolutely, I always regret it every time I have to choose a discipline in this industry because I always want to do it all. If it was left up to me it would all be mine. It wouldn't work, but it'd be mine. I've done it better than everyone else in my head, but the reality is totally different games. Development is fundamentally a collaborative process and you have to be able to let other people get involved and help them get involved in order to achieve the best results. It's a kind of a watershed moment when you realise that although you are an egotistical swine, you can't actually do it alone. There are actually people who are better than you and they can do things better and when you let them and help them to do their jobs, then you get the best result from a games company"

KIM

"That said, back in the day when I started in games design at Gremlin it was literally big sheets of paper and coloured pens. I drew the map and I said this happens here when you do this and I gave it to the programmer and it was awesome! The trick was I'd give it to the programmer and say I want this to happen here, but I don't think it's possible and they'd go, "Oh I'll be the judge of that and off they'd go""

So a couple of easy questions to start with. Who have you worked for in the industry? What do you actually do?

KIM

"Right, O.K. well I started at Gremlin as a designer and became an associate producer/project manager because I was marginally more organised than everyone else. I was also about ten years older than everyone else which was helpful. Gremlin was eventually brought out by Infogram. I left Gremlin at that point, shortly before they crashed and burned and went to work at Particle Systems, another small indie developer in Sheffield. I worked for them for about 4 years I think and after a couple of years they got bought out by Argonauts and then Argonauts crashed and burned taking us down with them. Then I worked in a company in Sutton Coldfield and I was with them just under a year. They crashed and burned and at that point I very nearly left the industry, but I'm glad I didn't because I came to Blitz (for most of that era I was doing project management, I think my first team was 5 people and my penultimate team was about 45 people) (Blitz). My role was P.A. to Andrew Oliver, basically helping him organising development again. What I now do is work in P.R. partly organising us speaking at and attending conferences, but my heart lies with the educational side where I/we get to liaise with skill set and universities to try and improve the quality of education, so that we can get better and more talented people into the industry and again to make it obvious to people that there are careers available to them"

BECKY

"I started off at Evolution Studios working as Q.A. tester where I worked on the first three Motostorm games which was great fun, but they had a kind of very bad work ethic down there in that you were expected to do overtime pretty much all the time"

"So like a permanent crunch?"

BECKY

"Yeah, pretty much. It wasn't too bad because the whole studio would work on one game so there was at least a little bit of downtime at the end of each project, but your manager would say to you: "I need someone to do overtime so whose willing to do that?" They made out it was a voluntary thing, but if you didn't do it you got like a black mark against your name, even if you had a family or people you had to look after. So I got increasingly frustrated there at not being recognised for the hard work I had been doing, for the fact I was in constant crunch, that I was travelling a long distance to get there and they didn't seem to really care about that. So I started looking for jobs and saw Blitz come up and it seemed like a really fun place so I applied and started off in Q.A. here and that was awesome. A much friendlier environment where everybody seemed to be more focused on you. What you wanted and wanting to help you to progress in your career. We had a much friendlier environment here in Q.A. They expected you to work hard, but they didn't expect you to forget the rest of your life just for work. I then got offered the opportunity to work on The Biggest Loser game as a junior designer so I snapped that up pretty sharpish and since then I've worked on SpongeBob. Now I've moved on to another game and its really good fun, challenging and you get to do a lot of different things from the concept stage deciding what the game is actually going to be like, how it's going to work and then all the way through to implementing it and fixing things, which is what I like to do"

DARREN

"Blitz Games is my first industry job. I returned to college as a mature student, graduated and I've noticed that a common theme around this table is the statement I applied everywhere I could. I think that's one of the secrets (to landing a job) is to actually apply to places. I think that's the difference between those who make it and those who don't"

"I find it phenomenally interesting because when I started out there was no internet, you couldn't just search online for games companies"

DARREN

"I went on, I think, gamesdev.net and on there was a list of U.K. games developers and I just sent a disc to all of them"

JONATHAN

"Edge magazine"

ANDREW

"What I would say is that applying to everyone can work, but there is another case which works very well which is actually to choose someone (I did that). If you have a hero of a game development area you particularly want to work in, you just persistently batter them. I know people who have got into every company in the games industry just by deciding they want to work there and working consistently to get there, people who have gone to Valve, people who have gone to Rare. People in this industry really respect passion. If you just want to get in then applying everywhere works. If you do have somewhere that you want to go, if you have a specific goal in mind, then it's usually useful to talk to them. The industry is becoming a lot more open to engaging in those sort of conversations, we respect enthusiasm and if you do want to work for a specific company then just consistently kind of asking them am I there yet? What can I do to get there?"

JONATHAN

"Here's what I've done. Here's example of what I can do. Here's what I like to do. Could you just take five minutes and look at it. The fact people will go out of their way, if they're studying, working in another industry, whatever they're doing. The fact they're still doing it at home and they care enough to do it at home that is a massive thing, it really is"

So would you say having a good, polished, up to date show reel is the key?

DARREN

"Oh yes, Becky was saying dedication to a single company or dedication to multiple, just any kind of dedication is. There's this attitude of: "Oh I'll just do a course and get a job". You know the kind of casual: "I sent a couple of applications and I didn't get it". If you've got that attitude where you've sent one or two or even no applications, then you're not going to get in that way"

BECKY

"I think some graduates expect people to come to them. I think they feel "Oh I've got a degree, now everyone will come and give me a job" and it doesn't work like that"

Recently I've been talking to some students. Obviously the book is going to be marketed at that audience. There are people out there who believe just because they're doing a course in games design, animation or code they will definitely get a job out of it. It's almost heartbreaking to say well if you work hard and really set it as your goal then you will, but it is a highly competitive industry.

DARREN

"When we talk to the students on the open day and I do portfolio reviews the one thing I say to them is: "It's up to you to convince these people to give you a job, they have got hundreds of students coming at them. They are the ones with the jobs. They don't need to make an effort""

JONATHAN

"They can cherry pick, they're not desperate"

DARREN

"It's up to you to make it as easy as possible for them to hire you over anyone else"

A good example of this is the last Q.A. role I had to open. I didn't advertise and I had 60 C.V.s on my desk ready to check through without me needing to do anything.

DARREN

"It is tough out there especially with the recession. You have a lot of industry veterans out there going for the same jobs as well"

ANDREW

"You see you say that, but actually right now if I could have five programmers who would fit into my team, I would hire every single one of them. I actually could do with those right now. The difference between whether you get in, I think you touched on this Darren, the difference is basically the easy stuff. It's the easy stuff in my experience that I think that graduates generally forget. A lot of people say the games industry doesn't engage with people, but you have to look at the PUBLIC WORK we put out, it's really easy to figure out which games company has been responsible for authoring what work. It's also really easy to get your hands on looking at that work to see whether or not that type of game is something that you're interested in. One of the classic mistakes people have with their first couple of jobs in the industry is to go and work for a company whose games they have absolutely no interest in because they happen to have the words "computer games". A lot of companies out there that make gambling games that are used in pubs, some people are interested in that, some people are not interested in that, some people are interested in racing games, some people are not interested in those, some people are interested in massively multiplayer games, some people are not interested in those. If your focus is specific or if it's narrow, it doesn't have to be by a genre if you work in an area like Darren. What you wanted is artistic freedom to look at a whole range of different concepts"

DARREN

"It's actually more engaging for me to have variety and do something different each week"

ANDREW

"But you can understand that by the PUBLIC WORK that a games company has put out. If you turn up for an interview without having played our games, at least one of them, that will basically go down as a massive cross against your name because you don't know what you're letting yourself in for. If you don't understand the work we are doing then you have put a distance between yourself and that position. By engaging with the PUBLIC WORK that a games company has put out you reduce that distance, you make it easier for us to start imagining how you would work with in a team. That doesn't take a degree, that actually takes about half an hour/an hour or so of playing games from a library if nothing else. So that's my recommendation, reduce the distance from you and your employer and don't just throw out C.V.s once you're qualified. Actually spend a little bit of time with the companies that you're asking to massively invest in you. Invest in seeing whether they will actually work for you. If you live on the other side of the country and you're not prepared to relocate to come to that company then you have to think about whether that's actually going to work for you. If you have never played their games or their games are not of interest to you (some of this is general job hunting, but a lot of this is specific to us), if you don't like the games we make and if you hate them or think they're rubbish, would you be happy here? Possibly not and I've had this in several companies trying to get people in who do not like the games we're making they don't like them and they have no enthusiasm then they don't like their job, SURPRISE!"

An artist friend of mine moved out of traditional games (after many years) because he was bored of drawing bullet holes in everything which I think is a good example of that. Just going back to the portfolio reviews, have you ever seen a portfolio and thought: "Wow I have to hire this guy?"

DARREN

"Yeah, we have open days every year"

KIM

"At least three"

DARREN

"In total I think we get about 20 – 30 artists that we actually accept to look at and review. In amongst them, there is usually a couple which are just like "Wow this artist is certainly worth consideration""

KIM

"And these are people who haven't even finished their degrees yet"

So if you were in that position, you're maybe a year and a half into a two/three year course and you come along to an open day and the guys on the other end of the table really love your work, what would you advise to a student at that point?

DARREN

"I'd tell them to take it!"

KIM

"I wouldn't. I'd say go and finish your degree"

DARREN

"I'd say take it. I've never been asked for my certificate. My portfolio has got me everywhere. This is purely 2D art. I can only speak about 2D art"

Is it fair to say it depends on the discipline? I asked

EVERYONE

"Yes"

ANDREW

"I think if it's a programmer or a technical member of staff I'd advise what Kim is saying. It's funny because nobody ever does actually look at your degree"

KIM

"Not in our industry, but what I'm thinking (and actually you are quite right if you have a portfolio then anywhere you go that's purely what you'll be judged on) is that for example if you're a coder and you spend some time in the industry without completing your degree (somebody snaps you up), but then a few years down the line you want to move into something else, other places will require bits of paper. I think it's extremely hard now to become a programmer without going through a university course, just because the levels of skills required, the level of knowledge required is so high, it's not impossible that someone could teach themselves that, but it is very unlikely. Art much easier perhaps, design much easier, design actually we don't care what qualifications you have, we only care that you can make interesting games and show them to us and talk us through them that would get you an interview!"

I'm struggling to think of any designers I've met who didn't start in Q.A.

JONATHAN

"It does happen"

KIM

"We have at least three people that we have recruited from game design courses"

JONATHAN

"It's changing now because of the game design courses which are becoming more popular. I'd just like to go back to a point Darren was making, if you're good enough with half a year to go (on your course) then you'll still be good enough half a year later. There is no point throwing it all in you just make yourself look like a loser. You've thrown it in! I can't rely on you now, what are you going to do half way through a project? You'll just quit, I want someone I can rely on as well"

So as a potential recruiter would you look at that (throwing in the course) and say well will this guy be able to survive crunch?

JONATHAN

"One hundred percent"

Will they dash off? When you need them the most because that's when things start getting really hard.

JONATHAN

"Absolutely and that does happen in the games industry all the time. It's not all sweets and lights, it's not all: "Yea we're making computer games aren't we lucky". There's sixty percent of the time when it's "Bugger me this is a pain in the ass! Half nine at night and I've got to write reams and reams of documentation that no one ever reads and I can't just turn around and go I can't be bothered to finish that"

So one of the things some of the other interviewees have touched upon, is a career in games over glamorised?

VARIOUS

"Yes"

"Absolutely"

"Highly"

SIMON

"I think they should put out health warnings"

BECKY

"Disclaimers"

SIMON

"Disclaimers to say we need problem solvers, because that's what we're doing, we're problem solvers, every day"

KIM

"I think there's a massive misunderstanding. At one end of the spectrum you have people who say "You play games all day and have no concept of the extremely tricky and technical skills required" and at the other end it's the "Oh how wonderful" without looking at the fact that it's very hard work. It's not that well paid, it's not bad but it's not that well paid and there are quality of life issues. Certainly in the U.K. I think there are a lot of more mature companies who are addressing those issues and I think the ones who are addressing it are generally the ones which are still around and the ones who didn't address those issues have died and rightly so in some ways."

So do any of you regret working in games?

ANDREW

"There have been times where I have. I think the interesting thing about games which everyone says, you're on the cutting edge, you're solving problems that have never been solved before, it's amazing you're doing things that people have never done before. The flip side of that is when it's two o'clock in the morning and you're sat on your own with your machine trying to solve a problem which has never been solved before and you wonder what will happen to everybody's jobs or the project around you if you do not solve the problem (that has never been solved before) and you can't even explain it to somebody because it is so complicated, then there is an enormous amount of stress and investment there. The good companies, the ones that Kim was talking about, are the ones that don't put you in that position. However, it does happen everywhere and I think you cannot underestimate the amount of intensive hard work involved in kind of doing that and stress. It is quite a stressful business for everybody involved. I don't think there is anyone, in any role, anywhere in the industry that does not get pushed on with the thumb of pressure for limited periods of time at some point during development. It's kind of hard because that bit is never explained to you as you come in the doors i.e. that it will be this painful. I can't think of another industry that would ever manage to do this to their people. One of the good things that we have in our company is that we try our absolute damndest to work around this, but sometimes when you're doing something new and you're doing it on a very restrictive form of financing (if we were in the aerospace or the defence industry they'd be throwing billions at us to solve these problems), but we don't have that money and we still have to solve them, in some ways we use work around it and use magicians tricks to get around the problem"

Dirty hack is a phrase that springs to mind.

ANDREW

"Dirty hack is the absolute phrase. It is the gold standard of two a.m. problem solving, but it will come down to you. You need to be responsible, you need to be reliable, you need to be hard working and you need to be very determined. These are all qualities that we admire, probably above degrees"

KIM

"I have to say, although I don't regret working in games, I am very grateful that I'm no longer a project manager because that's a stressful job (as they all are). Project managers/producers have always had a bad name in the industry, people say you don't need them, they don't do anything, yeah that's right!"

JONATHAN

"That is right, that is true! There are different areas of pressure for everybody. You've got the problem area of solving a huge problem, an insurmountable mountain and you've also got the problem of creating. It's different for design and art, you've got to come up with a load of ideas for Barbie Horse Riding Adventures. I couldn't give a s**t about Barbie and her horse riding adventures, but I have to now and I have to lock myself in it"

DARREN

"I think it's more like Andrew talks about solving problems people have never solved before. In 2D art we're very lucky, design and programming are kind of new things.

In 2D art we have several thousands of years of guys who have done this. There usually is a solution"

JONATHAN

"But you still have to get excited about things you don't care about"

DARREN

"Well yeah, but what we have as well and what we all have is that we're paid to be creative and if you have a bad day, well 2D artists sometime get a day where their hand will just not do what they tell it and they really can't draw and they go "Oh I can't draw today" If you're at college you can just go, phone in sick or something like that, but here you have got to come in, you've got to work, you've got to keep pushing, you've got to draw"

JONATHAN

"That's what really separates out the truly creative people, you cannot just go click (on the computer) I'm off now. With Barbie Horse Adventure you have to be "This is awesome!" You can stroke the mane and look at her jumping over stuff and you're off and away. Everyone looks at you and are like what are you on about and you're like trust me!"

Can I just ask did you work on Barbie Horse Adventures?

JONATHAN

"I did work on Barbie Horse Adventures"

BECKY

"Can you tell?"

For years I've used that as an example of a terrible game to work on or a game you wouldn't want to work on.

JONATHAN

"Well you wouldn't want to work on it, but you can't work on Call of Duty all the time!"

KIM

"I think a lot of people who say that they want to work in games actually want to work on Halo and when you explain to them that this game is actually aimed at six to twelve year old children or six to twelve year old girls, they go that's not cool"

JONATHAN

"Or I'm not interested in that"

KIM

"Then actually we don't want you, we really don't want you. We want the people who will go "Oh wow! How do I make that fun for the target audience?" Not for the guy in Edge magazine. It's a really bad pun, but it is horses for courses"

BECKY

"That's one of the first questions you get asked. When I'm talking to people in the pubs or to my little nephews, what games have you worked on? Have you worked on COD, have you worked on Halo?"

JONATHAN

"Did you make Tomb Raider?"

BECKY

"Did you make Tomb Raider, no!"

ANDREW

"I think everyone's got some of those awful projects, well not awful because they were bad, but awful because you were located (on to the project) and you kind of have to push through that. I personally hate football, I've hated football since I was a kid and yet through the mystical forces that sometimes move us around projects I found myself working on a football management game, a very long time ago and I had to learn every single rule of football. Down to the last specific detail things that sometimes even football fans aren't aware of themselves. I had to learn every single league, club, trophy that was available and I had to learn to programme those inside out. I spent a lot of the time on that project crying on the inside, sometimes on the outside as well, when the lights were down low." he joked and then continuing his point "but as Jon said you have to put yourself to one side at that point and work on the game for the target audience, which is not you!"

It becomes more of a job rather than a passionate element of your job, I added.

KIM

"It's being professional, being professional is being able to be passionate about something you don't necessarily want to play yourself"

I hate football as well and had to test a F.I.F.A. game and I've never worked so hard on a front end and menu system in my life. All day, everyday how am I going to break the menu system? Because I just couldn't stand playing the actual game! Which kind of brings us nicely to the next question, what is the highlight and lowlight of your career?

JONATHAN

"I can't deal with the lowlight, but the highlight is being here with you today"

Have you considered a role in P.R.?

DARREN

"I think for me, when I first started at Blitz and the team that was making Dead to Rights was in pre-development. They didn't have a concept artist at the time and although I was brought in for the pitch team, it was a case of we have nothing for you to do so we're going to give you to another team for a couple of months and you're going to help out with Dead to Rights on the pre-dev. It was the first game I ever worked on, in my first job in the industry and about four years later it's due to come out. I'd been on pitch, but then towards the end of it (the project) we needed some standing art. There was some in-game advertising on billboards which was going to come through on Xbox live, but what we needed was placeholder art for people who didn't have Xbox live so there wasn't just a bunch of blank billboards (for these people), so me and some of the other guys did some posters for this. I remember seeing a preview of Dead to Rights on a games programme and the character ran past one of my posters. It was like that's my art! In my game! Because it was my first game I was being selfish, it was my game. So seeing my art in my game on the telly was just fantastic"

It's like the first time you see your name in the credits, up on screen

JONATHAN

"I still had my first game in cellophane and a mate picks it up, goes: "Oh what is this? It looks s**t" and opened it, I was shocked: "You've taken it out of the cellophane!!""

ANDREW

"I think it is those moments when you see your work. Professionally I remember all the number one's that come out and you go: "Oh this is number one across Europe, which means how many hundred thousands, oh we're into millions so that's 1.5 million people! Oh I wish I had really done that a bit better". Then you kind of get bigger again and you go: "Oh, O.K. so more and more people are playing this". You realise what an effect your work has had on such a large number of people's lives. Those are the best personal achievements"

JONATHAN

"Someone emailed me about a game we made and it was like I've got a question about blah, blah and blah. So I answered that and he replied: "Thanks for that. This is my favourite game of all time." Somewhere in the world there isn't a cynical bastard, there is someone who says I got pleasure from something that you worked on and you show it to everyone else and say look this person really liked the game"

BECKY

"That's really a good point, on The Biggest Loser, we had people email us. The Biggest Loser is a fitness game, I don't know if you've seen the TV show. You've probably heard of it, so people have to lose a lot of weight (in the game) and people were emailing and saying this game has literally changed my life and that's just awesome! Plus we got to see it on TV in America it was on the actual Biggest Loser TV show and I saw my game that I'd been working on, on TV in America! I was just gobsmacked"

JONATHAN

"I once went out to America and stood next to and spoke to Michael Phelps, the guy has won so many gold medals he doesn't know what to do with them. I was like how did I ever get to be standing next to Michael Phelps? Those kinds of things are just amazing, you wouldn't get that anywhere else!"

SIMON

"I think even more than that for me it's the amount of autonomy and creativity that you've got within the studio. You can get to fulfil your creative needs as an artist. Speaking as artist in both 2D and 3D, there's a lot of people that ask me what do you do, do you get to draw and I'm like YEAH! From the time I was little (2/3) I've always been an artist, I've always drawn and my parents have always said I was doing something artistic because being artistic is how I've always been. So to be able to be in an atmosphere where there are a lot of people around you who can not only look at your work and critique it, so you're getting better, but that also you're part of this team that is just making something which outstanding. Something that people can play through (and that's the beauty of working on something that's not static), get so much enjoyment out of it, on so many different levels. That's why it doesn't matter to me what type of game I'm working on at all because I see every game that I'm working on as a challenge and my challenge is to make them look as good as they possibly can be. So sometimes I'll be going around making visual judgements and saying: "Oh I think that's worked really well there", because my whole thing is whatever I'm doing or whatever I'm associated with I want it to be brilliant, I want it to be great! That's the beauty of working within the games companies because you get your chance to put that little bit forward and make something look, feel better!"

BECKY

"It's the enthusiasm of some of the people here. I think it really kind of drives you along, when you see other people get excited then that helps you to get even more excited about it, like an endless cycle"

KIM

"I'm not going to say that in itself it's the saviour of companies, but I think that any company that does not have that attitude now will die, because it is so competitive! You just have to look at the quality of the art and the technical side games companies are at now. We have to compete with that every single game we make and I think young people do need to understand that if they're an artist they need to be looking at the big games and asking how far off of that am I and how do I get there? Of course it's going to be completely terrifying when you're fifteen because you're not going to be very good. But that's where a lot of our guys started once and now they're awesome!"

DARREN

"I remember when I was a mature student and someone tipped me off to conceptart.org, which is a big website. I went on there and I started clicking through and you've got my competition from basically the rest of the world who want to get into games and there is some AMAZING talent up on there. My first instinct was s**t I've got to raise my game! It' wasn't like I'm never going to make it. It was like: "Wow this is where I need to be. In the top ten percent of these guys""

JONATHAN

"It's what I tell my designers, you have to live, breathe and believe it. You have to be that person, what's the best thing I can be? What's the best thing I can think of? You have to aspire to that to be the person who get's on!"

A friend of mine once said to me (he's been in the industry for fifteen/sixteen years) it took me about ten years to realise that Q.A. were not criticising me.

BECKY

"That's a very good point"

That they're saying to me: "You can improve this". In essence to raise my own bar on the work I produce. Do you agree? Do you kind of feel that Q.A. can be motivational and de-motivational at the same time? After all we will give you six hundred bugs to finish off two weeks before the end of a project

JONATHAN

"Q.A. is tough. It's a hard job. You've got to have your head switched on to do proper Q.A. but also it gets a bad press within the industry for some reason. It is seen as the starting block if you don't know what you're doing, but then you move off and I think that's the wrong way to view it. I don't agree with that, maybe it's where the attitude of: "You don't tell me what to do" comes from. But nine times out of ten people in Q.A. are gamers, they've spent all of their free time playing games so they know what they like and what they don't like and if they have something to say by all means listen to it. Sometimes their timing can be off, making suggestions at the end of a project, we're in master now and you're still coming up with suggestions"

BECKY

"They are looked down upon in certain places, the bottom rung and they don't know what they're doing. I think that's where that attitude comes from really"

ANDREW

"I think the industry is changing. I remember ten years ago, Q.A. was looked upon as being the people we got from the chip shop when we needed to test the game. It's true a lot of the Q.A. people were paid hourly, because they would be shipped out as soon as the project ended"

BECKY

"But now it is being seen more as a career choice"

ANDREW

"But now I'd never in a million years think about approaching the start of a game development without fundamentally thinking about where Q.A. are going to contribute to it and exactly in what ways we can get them to be more involved, because they are so valuable, utterly valuable. We now have them (certainly on my team) internally within the team, working with the team constantly looking at various areas, not just the current bugs within the build or anything like that. They look at quality matrix from play testing. They look at comparisons with other games. They do huge amounts of work for us and when we engage with them we get so much more out of them. So as somebody who's reasonably high up in a large team I have the utmost respect for Q.A. and I'd never allow it if I heard any of the people I manage disparaging Q.A. in any way, shape or form then they would get a good kicking off me"

BECKY

"I think there is an external problem as well, in that people who are outside of the industry see Q.A. as sitting around playing games all day. So you do have people applying who have not the slightest bit of interest in finding bugs, they just want to sit around and ass about all day I think that is a big problem sort of breaking down that stereotype, that it's actually a job and you have to do really well to get the best sort of product at the end of it"

DARREN

"I think it's interesting a point Jon made about it being seen as a stepping stone type of job. I was brought in as an artist, my manager didn't sit me down and say in six months time we'll make you a designer/get you to do some programming! I was brought in as an artist and this is what I was going to do and this attitude that Q.A. is basically treading water until their actual job frees up, probably contributes to the kind of they're not taken seriously attitude"

ANDREW

"I think a lot of that's because they're contractors, they do have to migrate and so I guess they're generally they're not as persistent within the team and that's been a mistake. Previously you kind of ramp up a Q.A. team for a few months and then you cut them off and send them back to the chip shop or to go on to working in banks or whatever their proper job is going to be. But nowadays that's not so much the case. We tend to have strong Q.A. managers who don't allow time wasters within their team, who don't allow the: "Oh yeah I'll play a game for an hour or so". Managers who don't allow those people in and if somehow they do get in, they get them out equally as quickly and actually reserve those places for the people with the dedication, commitment and reliability that we admire and from that point of view it all becomes plain sailing. I think Q.A. within the industry is building on that and building on the fact that it's more of a profession"

JONATHAN

"Five years ago, ten years ago, if you wanted to be a designer, how could you prove it? There was no way if you hadn't worked anywhere else. There was no way of proving you could be a designer. Design is one of those things a lot of people think everyone can do design and a lot of creative people can design, there are also a lot of people that really can't, but how do you prove that? The classic way was getting into Q.A., starting off by making suggestion here and there and understanding how games actually work, how games are actually created and made and moving forward from there. So it was almost like you had to do your education, then prove yourself before you could be a designer. There were very few instances that went education then designer, you could go education to be a programmer or an artist, it works in those ways, but not a designer. That's why you have this: "You have to do your stint in Q.A.", you have to do your stint as a private before you can be decorated"

So I discussed a fair bit about Q.A. It's what I've done for over ten years and it's still seen as a foot in the door to lead onto better things and I do say that it is possible (most of the designers I know started out in Q.A.), but at the same time I mention that I don't want people to disregard a career in Q.A. in its own right. I guess my question is it (Q.A.) still viable as both or is it becoming a case of now that we have all these really good on the ball courses perhaps Q.A. as a learning area might be no more.

BECKY

"I think it's still vital, to be honest, to learn how the industry works and to learn how a game is made. I never did a games design course so I don't really know what they do, but my impression is that they don't actually teach you a lot of skills you'll need on the job. You learn that by coming in and working your way through"

KIM

"Most game design courses are very poor"

DARREN

"As Jon said a few years back most games designers came through Q.A. I can't vouch for game design courses because I'm an artist, but there's certainly (the unreal engine is now free to use, there's unity, there's flash) a lot of ways for students to make their own games and I think that's certainly another way designers can get experience and make themselves as an interview prospect more interesting. Especially if they come in with a prototype or a game they've made"

ANDREW

"They're valuable skills as well! Q.A. skills are valuable. I've got a programmer on my team (a brilliant programmer) who was a Q.A. technician. He started off that way and then decided that he wanted to become a programmer so he taught himself how to code. He is now a really good programmer on my team. I think the interesting thing is that most people in this room are developers and generally they come from development backgrounds and we're quite focused on individual disciplines as a group. If you go a little bit higher than us, then the skills of that layer (producers/project directors) are different they have a whole raft of things they need to do e.g. finance and all sorts of other horrible things (client management), but their skill set also includes a portion of the skill set that the Q.A. staff are taught. If you didn't go through Q.A. then you have to learn that skill set for yourself. The ability to test, validate, analyse and figure out exactly where something is different and be able to specify that and communicate it to other people are the skills that good project managers and the people above us in the industry have. So it kind of comes around again I think to the fact that if you've had time in Q.A. then you're setting yourself up for jumping even higher. I know a lot of people in Q.A. who have jumped up directly from Q.A. to the project director/the producer positions. Although we're are quite a flat industry in terms of hierarchy and everyone has a role and respect in the team, there's a lot of different routes and one that we don't tend to discuss often enough in these kinds of discussions is that of the project manager and Q.A. is an absolutely brilliant way of getting there"

KIM

"That's very true. We have a list somewhere on one of the open day slides that includes all of the positions (that we know of) where people have gone through Q.A. and it's pretty much the full spectrum of all the disciplines. I think it's going to continue like that. I think if people want to come into Q.A. and stay there FANTASTIC, if that's what they're good at then it's brilliant, but if we have one guy who does it for a bit and then says actually I want to do this, then go for it (certainly on the management side)"

So would you all recommend it? As a place to get your foot in and learn a bit, see how games are made and take it from there.

ANDREW

"Particularly if you're not decided. I think that if you are absolutely precise and know exactly what you want to do with laser like clarity i.e. you want to be the world's best artist and you have the portfolio to back it up and you definitely want to work on role playing games at a certain company, then Q.A. probably isn't the path for you, but if you're not sure then Q.A. is the way"

JONATHAN

"I know plenty of people who have made a huge success out of being from Q.A. and with nowadays people outsourcing more stuff, outsourcing Q.A. I'd imagine, Q.A. is just going to get bigger and bigger and it should occur to the industry to realise that quality is first"

KIM

"There's another benefit that I mention to the students, because they (Q.A.) are on short term contracts you can actually go around and sample a number of companies before deciding which one you want to work for."

"The differences between a publisher and a developer, a racing studio over a music studio" I replied.

KIM

"Absolutely and also the company culture I can speak from personal experience from a previous company where they were working on a licence that I absolutely adored; I have to work on that! Ignoring the fact that there were serious management problems, which came back to bite me. However if I had paid more attention to the company culture and ethos I might not have been so quick to stitch myself up. When talking about people who want to work in the industry and their expectations there are currently something like 8,000 actual developers in the U.K., that's not counting distribution and publishing and all the rest of it, the actual people who hands on make games. However many courses are turning out people it is massively, massively competitive! I don't know how we get this across because at the same time we don't want to put people off with: "It's an impossible peak to climb", but it is highly competitive. Also now the other side are indie developers. There is absolutely nothing stopping them making an IOS game, an android game, a little flash game and getting it out there"

DARREN

"I think the lesson or the message to students is (as Andy mentioned earlier) be the best! Be in that group that are at the top! With 2D art at least I would recommend doing an art course, a lot of game courses come under the bracket of media and you're not taught art. I would say do an art foundation course, possibly an art degree".

KIM

"Learn to draw"

DARREN

"Learn to draw, get additional skills if, you know, get good at art. It's a lot more use than it would be doing a games course"

SIMON

"Absolutely"

"You can do the games course as well, if you've got the time and the money"

So it's about setting the bar high, maximising the effort.

DARREN

"No one is going to give you a leg- up. You have got to go and get it"

KIM

"And I think we should also bang the drum for soft skills. So (although we kind of touched upon this) make it easy for us to see your work. If you put your work on a website make it nice and clearly designed"

DARREN

"No more than three clicks to see my art"

I've had candidates with half-finished show reels or ones with: "It's a few years out of date; it's not the best reflection of my work"

DARREN

"Well if you're not going to make the effort why would I?"

KIM

"If it's not the best reflection of your work, then why are you showing it to me? I only want to see the best"

I've been meaning to update it for a while

DARREN

"We were planning on giving you that really good job, but now we won't, we'll just give you the rubbish one"

KIM

"Be courteous, be clear, have good communication skills, because you're going to be working with people who see the world in radically different ways. I was thinking when we were talking about (what I consider to be a very old fashioned attitude to) Q.A. there was also the very old fashioned coder/artist. That pretty much doesn't exist anymore and it doesn't exist because everyone knows they have to work together and that the coders create the tools that the artists have to use. Therefore the more communication that goes on, the better tools we get, the better work we get and the happier people we get"

JONATHAN

"A lot of people who want to work in the games industry are what I'd call geeks. So the communication is ever so important, especially for a designer. You have to be able to get your ideas and your views across clearly and concisely so that other people can understand. If you're a shrinking violet you need to take steps to address that. I think there's that mentality of: "I code in my bedroom, I don't need to talk to people", but those days have gone, you really need to get out of that mindset as well. I think that's a really important thing"

Certainly I've always found it a lovely thing that no matter what company I've ended up in or whatever arguments I may get into over a project, you can always find common ground because you're all from that sort of gaming, comic books, sci-fi background.

DARREN

"I used to explain that one of the best things about this job is that I can make a joke without having to explain what I mean. When I worked in a call centre you'd have to, whereas here there's that shared history"

JONATHAN

"But the way the games industry is changing and evolving you have to be more aware, more expressive I think as well. You need to be able to cover all the bases"

KIM

"Definitely"

So have any of you guys done anything unique to get into the industry?

DARREN

"I made my demo disc, basically it was very clear, easy to navigate, no more than three clicks to see a large image of my artwork. I also had artwork on my C.V., my C.V. was clear, well presented, spell checked and with a bit of graphical design. From what I hear that's pretty unique for 2D artists, so just simple obvious stuff. I heard a story about some artist who got a job with a trendy magazine in London by sending them jelly babies nailed to crucifixes. Just make it look a little different and make yourself look professional, make yourself look like you can do the job."

JONATHAN

"I did hear a story about a friend of mine who now works in the television industry. He was applying for a job and he asked to see this chap. The secretary wrote back apologising saying he didn't have enough time in his schedule to see him. So he (the friend) wrote back and gave him ten different things to do that would save him a few minutes in his day. Wear a clip on tie, this will save you x amount of time; wear Velcro shoes, so he didn't have to tie his shoes in the morning. There you go, that's enough time for my meeting and it worked. He now does Dragons Den (TV show). I had an argument with a guy who was interviewing me when I first joined Codemasters and that seemed to work well purely because he was that kind of person and he enjoyed the fact that I questioned something and argued back"

You weren't willing to change your view just because it was an interviewer

KIM

"I have a slightly contentious one which is being female is actually a massive plus because most companies want more women in their work force. We are aware that we are very unbalanced and after that (getting hired) you rise and fall by your own methods. I don't think I've seen women promoted (with the possibility of one exception) beyond what they can do, in fact quite the reverse. There's certainly been traditionally a lot of sexism in the industry, not from the developers interestingly enough but in my experience from management. That was my experience in the past, not here. Also my situation was odd because I was in my mid thirties when I got into the industry and I was working with a lot of lads in their early twenties so I had a kind of existing authority which was extremely useful. I was a massive geek and I swore like a trooper (both of these things helped). However, I think that just going to an interview if you are an intelligent woman who can clearly do the job you will have a huge advantage because we're looking to even up the numbers. Of course not all companies think that way"

JONATHAN

"Well I hired Becky and it was nothing to do with the fact she was a girl. It might help to even the odds up a little"

KIM

"I think it helps to get the interview and not the job"

BECKY

"Because you stand out more"

KIM

"Yes that's what I mean"

So do you think attitudes to women are changing, have changed or are in that kind of process?

JONATHAN

"I think that whole attitude or anything like that is changing"

KIM

"I think it's really hard to tell"

BECKY

"It's more hidden now, I think. I've still had recent experiences that have been quite upsetting. I think a lot of people generally are thinking of women as equals, but there are still people around who are just going through the motions and underneath they don't really believe that you are. You can tell that when you get into a deep conversation with someone by the things that they say. So it' still there, but it is getting better, it's got better even since I started working in the industry, but I think it still underlines some people's attitudes"

JOANTHAN

"That's just society in general"

KIM

"And I think it varies from studio to studio. There are certain studios which are still very clearly boy's clubs"

JONATHAN

"Again it goes back to that programming in my bedroom mentality. Why socialise with a wide spectrum of people? Am I comfortable with a wide section of people? If you're not find a company where you're welcomed"

KIM

"But I also think, what's amazing to me I can remember thinking when I was at Gremlin that this would be   a very hard industry for anyone gay to come out in and we have two out gay people at Blitz which I think is FANTASTIC! But I'm also very aware that that is very dependent on who you work with and, as you say, society in general"

I think it's interesting to try and distinguish. Is that the industry or is that kind of the attitude to homosexuality at that time?

KIM

"Exactly"

BECKY

"It's probably because in society women aren't expected to do a lot of things, gay people aren't expected to do certain things and that kind of spills over into the industry. People can think how they were brought up to think and it can be very difficult to break out of that"

JONATHAN

"I'd like to think that people in the games industry are more intelligent than that"

But there's no getting around it, as an industry we didn't even perceive females as a customer base until within the last few years and it was just boys making toys for boys.

DARREN

"I remember when my mum came down to visit me. She met me one lunchtime and she was saying she could spot our lot and it was like 25-35 male, wearing a slogan t-shirt, jeans and trainers"

KIM

"Developers look like developers, anywhere in the world..."

Coming here today, it was only seeing the half a dozen people having a cigarette around the corner that made me think I must be nearby.

DARREN

"I think that's the point, it's like a lot of these attitudes. There is a certain type of person that becomes a games developer and that's shifting"

JONATHAN

"It needs to as well"

DARREN

"Well there is that core, that very typical kind of lad 25-35, male. It's almost like when they were pushing the Playstation One, it's the kind of demographic that they aimed at. It became a lad's accessory and I think it's very much that the industry is changing from that, but it's also still got that perception"

KIM

"Also the public's got that perception as well, which isn't helping. The sort of massively male dominated online forums, full of frothing fan boys. But one of the most interesting things you can do is logon to the Cosmopolitan (magazine), go to their forums and there is a thread there (now this is Cosmopolitan and I haven't read the magazine in years, it's just a glossy). This is an absolutely main stream women girly stuff and there you will find pages and pages of women saying I'm playing this, I used to play that, I play Left for Dead with my boyfriend, they play everything. Survival horror massively popular, but they play everything and they talk about it and I'm going: "This is really interesting because none of the rest of us have noticed this.""

DARREN

"Do they review games in Cosmopolitan?"

KIM

"No I don't think so, these are just readers who go on the forums. Have an interest in games, who are gamers. They found each other and they discuss what they're playing"

In a way a forum of that nature is almost a safe place for girls to discuss games where as we all know if you went on IGN, 1-up or any of those kind of forums it'd be a very different case.

DARREN

"If you buy Maxim, Total Film or any magazine aimed at men, DVD's will be reviewed, books will be reviewed, films will be reviewed and games will be reviewed. It's not just us saying girls don't play games"

KIM

"It's the rest of society as well, it's kind of like this quite large underground of women who play games and talk to each other about it secretly online"

SIMON

"I think I kind of bucked the trend as well, because there are very few black guys in the industry"

KIM

"Absolutely"

SIMON

"We've got I think two other black guys in this company. The thing is (as well) you see that in all the companies I've worked in I'm one of the only black guys there. I think possibly two others max and the thing is I don't know why that is"

You are bang on though. I've never given it much thought, but now you mention it I can think of maybe half a dozen people I know maybe who fall into that category

SIMON

"I always get a lot of young people, kids asking me games industry it looks fantastic how can I get in? I give them the spiel and tell them the hard stuff that you have got to go through to get in, but I just have a big question mark over why. Because I know I'm not the only person."

Do you think there's a role for an organisation in a similar vein to women in games, but for people of minorities and ethnicity?

SIMON

"I'm trying to work out if it's a cultural thing. I'm from a very lucky background in the fact that my parents saw that I was good at art and I always pursued it. However I know a lot of people I've grown up with whose parents have always been you will never get a job in art!"

KIM

"I think it's partly a generational thing. One of the things that I find frustrating and that I particularly try to tell people of my age who have teenage kids is that it is possible for the first time in five hundred years to earn a living as an artist! It's a proper job, it's got a pension and everything"

JONATHAN

"Kids can say I'm going to go make video games and parents will now say: "Oh fair enough" It is a legitimate job! I'd like to think it's more generational than any kind of malice towards anyone"

DARREN

"A couple of Christmases ago I totally went off on one of my aunt's new husband. His sister's son is about seven or eight and he's a very good quiet kid who basically spends all day drawing monsters and dinosaurs and stuff. He's absolutely fascinated by it and they'd just wish he'd stop that, be normal and mix with the other kids. I had a bit to drink and I totally went off on him because that was me like thirty years ago. I was the quiet kid and now I get paid, I've got a pension, I've got health insurance and it's like when I tell people I make games I have to explain I get paid to do it"

JOANTHAN

"With regards to the generational thing I think you just have to keep batting at it and then it becomes the norm and stops becoming an issue, the colour you are, the sex you are, your sexual orientation, how much hair you've got or not got it just becomes irrelevant"

Since we're basically out of time, any advice for people wanting to get in the industry today?

SIMON

"Work hard"

BECKY

"Be passionate"

DARREN

"For those who don't know people in the industry (especially artists), get online, get on forums. It's easy to find and get out there because there are people from the industry out there and in that way you will get to know people within the industry, talk to them, listen to their requirements"

But then look at VGcats, Penny Arcade or CAD you can just love the industry without having to become involved with actual games development

DARREN

"For those who don't know people in the industry, get online. There are places where these people hang out"

KIM

"Even Linkedin for example, I don't accept friendship requests or links from students because there would be too many. But my profile is there, my details are there, so are any number of people I have worked with over the years and people I work with now. Go and look at that and that will tell you a great deal about the sort of people you should be looking to get in touch with"

DARREN

"I remember and I'm not going to mention by name, but there was this girl who didn't get in to an open day because we reviewed her work and basically had more, higher quality applicants, she was under the quality threshold. She emailed Kim very politely and basically said can I maybe get some coaching or some feedback on my work. Kim's soft hearted so she asked around and I said: "Yeah send the stuff over to me, I'll take a look" and I ended up coaching this girl for six months. This was someone who wasn't good enough, who I had never met and I know (because we're friends) that she's now employed doing medical illustrations"

BECKY

"People are willing to help you if you just ask. Everyone is willing to give up five minutes of their time and give something a critique or career advice"

KIM

"Most of us are willing to help"

JONATHAN

"With designers it's about finding the magic in everything, find the magic in the games you love to play, find the magic in the games you don't like to play. Find the magic in bouncing a ball, why is that? Why do people play? Why do people have fun? It is all around you everywhere you look you can see the magic in things"

This actually came up in another designer interview. The interviewee recommended to literally bounce a ball off a wall and work out why it is fun, look at traditional board games and work out why it's fun, look at what people do in their spare time. If you want to design it's not just videogames.

KIM

"I always say to students go to the ballet, go to the opera, open yourself up to new things, don't just draw from the same geeky things that we all do. Travel, go and look at new things, go to museums"

BECKY

"It's that exploring mentality"

We can all pull resources form video games, we all know the greats and the Barbie Horse Adventures, but can we incorporate the fun from traditional games? I think that's a really good point to leave it on. I'd just like to thank you all for your time, it's been great meeting you and I for one have found it really interesting.

Chapter 4: Character Selection

Now that we know how games are made and what we need to do to hopefully gain employment, we should look at the individual job roles within the industry, what they're really like and what will aid your career more, experience or education. We'll also look at other aspects of the industry like the gender divide, the working hours and how all of this affects the people working in the industry. Let's explore the daily working life in the industry by looking at the roles themselves and what they're really like. Please keep in mind there are a huge amount of different roles in the industry and I couldn't possibly cover them all in this book, I've tried to give you a good mix of development roles and other types of roles in the industry, but this is by no means a comprehensive list.

> *Don't just know about your discipline (Audio, Art, Animation, Code, Design, Q.A., Production) get to know what the others do and how the whole team fits together. The more you know about the other disciplines the easier it will be to find solutions for what is in effect, the newest and most exciting industry of our age!*
>
> *-Nathan McCree*
> *Audio Director, Vatra Games*

Animation Department:

If it moves it's animated and the Animation Department deals with all moving elements within a game. As well as any moving content within a game (characters, plants, animals, weapons, etc.), they also work on the game's cut-scene's, lip-sync and any trailers or attract mode the game may use.

Roles: *Junior Animator, Animator, Lead Animator*

> *As an Animator, I was responsible for creating all animated sequences for the game. As I was an animator of a sprite based game, my animation work was 2D sprite based animations, which included a range of images that are then played in order to create the animated sequence.*
>
> *-Peter Clark*
> *VFX Artist, Codemasters*

Art Department:

Roles: *Junior Artist, Artist, Lead Artist, Head of Art*

The Art Department create the game's look, everything from the environment to the characters, the menus to the objects, all of it is created by the Art Department. Additionally the artists also create the concept artwork used in the pitching process.

> *I manage the art style of the game and work closely with the individual members of my team to ensure they are working efficiently, they are on style and the quality of work is maintained for all art going in game. I liaise with my Lead Coder and Lead Designer to ensure their art requirements are met and when I can tear myself away from meetings I contribute to the game's art directly, usually in a fairly strategic fashion.*
>
> *-Daniel Lodge*
> *Lead Artist, Doublesix Games*

Audio Department:

Sound (SFX) and music (BGM) all fall into the audio team's domain, these guys create and implement all sounds and music used in the title.

Roles: *Audio Engineer, Lead Audio Engineer, Head of Audio*

Well it usually starts with some idea for style. Sometimes it's very specific like "We want John Williams, Star Wars music", or "We want Edward Scissor Hands". Other times it can be vague and ambiguous. Then usually some temp track is put into the game to test the style. A temp track is a term we use for a piece of music that is classed as a placeholder. If the tests are successful and the Creative Director is happy then you can start to think about a composer. It may be you or it may be someone else who is more suited to producing that kind of style. A music brief is then put together and interviews take place. There are many different ways of implementing music into a game. So it's not always the same job.

-Nathan McCree
Audio Director, Vatra Games

Design Department:

The design team creates the game's story line, but this is just the beginning. They deal with a whole host of other things, making all the design decisions within the title. Every control method, level name or game rule has been chosen by the design team. The difficulty levels, the points within a level (re-spawn, weapons, health, etc.) are all carefully chosen by the designers.

Roles: *Junior Designer, Designer, Lead Designer, Assistant Director, Director*

As a game designer I'm responsible for all aspects of the game, from initial concept document through to the Game Design Document and post-production. This includes tasks such as narrative, level design, player character and A.I. design, U.I. flow, SFX, game mechanics, marketing and much, much more. I love the diversity that the job offers – from one day to the next I'll be doing completely different tasks, so I never get bored.

-Sophie Blackmore
Senior Designer, Rockstar Games

Production Department:

The production team is the central hub of any game. This team ensures the game is on track and within budget, they actively communicate between every department to ensure that from start to finish the whole process is tracked and on budget/target dates. Although all the central communication, planning and scheduling is done through the Production Department all departments communicate with each other and from time to time with the publisher.

Roles: *Assistant Producer, Producer, Executive Producer*

It's all about reacting to the needs of the project at any given time, as every project and team is different, so too are those needs. However, there are of course some consistencies, which might include attending one or more of the daily scrum meetings; doing a build review and distributing feedback and specific tasks based on it; liaising with the publisher about any outstanding issues or upcoming milestones; catching up with the EP and game director on problems and priorities; orchestrating the commission and distribution of any outsourced artwork; and one too many cigarette breaks.

-Jez Harris
Production Manager, Supermassive Games

Programming Department:

The Programming Department is the driving force behind any game studio. Everything in a game needs code to work, so this is one of the few teams who will work on a project from start to finish. As well as coding the game itself, they may also work on the studio tools for other departments or they may be found working in research and development creating new engines and tools for the next generation of games.

Roles: *Junior Coder, Coder, Lead Coder, Development Manager*

I'm a Lead Programmer so I write code for various systems. I architect systems, mentor juniors, work with other Leads.

-Rhys Twelves
Lead Programmer, Bioware

Quality Assurance Department:

The Quality Assurance (Q.A.) Department is responsible for the quality of the product. As well as testing the game itself, they will also help with balancing the difficulty of the game, checking the box and manual, localising the game into other languages and ensuring that the game passes the submission process. Additionally, they may also liaise with external test teams from the publisher and manage the bug database throughout all departments. It is often seen as a way into the industry, but should not be ignored as a possible career path in itself.

Roles: Junior Tester, Tester, Lead Tester, Q.A. Manager

My job is to break the game and make accurate records of how it was done so that the Development team can fix the issue. Sometimes this is easy as the bug will happen naturally, but then sometimes you have to really think about how you are going to force the game to break.

-Paul Sedgmore
Q.A. Manager, Colossal Games

Other departments:

There are so many people involved in a video game that I can't possibly mention them all here, many people make their living in or around the actual creation of the game. So many folk aid us in creating, marketing, managing and selling a game that it be wrong to think that a games career must involve development. To help give you some further roles to think about, I interviewed some friends of mine who help us to create the games, you can read the full interviews later on in this book.

Games journalist:

You read their reviews regularly, you've read the breaking news they present and they're the number one communication method between creating and consuming a game. So what does a games journalist actually do and how can you become one?

> *I do mostly news and features really, but also I do co-ordination of stuff for events with companies and things like that. So we'll sort out media partnerships or just arranging stuff with TIGA to get on board with their awards and various other things, so sort of relationship building as well. But day-to-day it's mostly writing news in the mornings, getting on with features stuff in the afternoons and occasionally getting on with more long term stuff.*
>
> *-Dan Pearson*
> *Senior Staff Writer, Gamesindustry.biz*

Recruitment agent:

The specialist recruitment agencies and agents provide a valuable service to the industry so what advice can they offer someone starting out in the industry?

> *Recruiters are really useful in a number of different ways, they manage your interviews, they are usually first to hear about new jobs or jobs that perhaps aren't public, they can give you vital advice on your C.V. and general career advice so I would say you could use a recruiter at any point.*
>
> *-Eamonn Mgherbi*
> *Managing Director, Avatar Games Recruitment*

P.R. Manager:

P.R. managers run all the publicity for the games we make, from when details are made public to how these details are presented everything comes through the P.R. manager.

> *I'm a publicist, which means it's my job to make sure that the games I work on are as visible as possible. If you read about one of my games and it's not an advert, I was almost definitely involved in that coverage in some way.*
>
> *-Leo Tan*
> *Senior P.R. Manager, Capcom*

Community Manager:

A Community Manager is often the public spokesperson for the game. These guys manage the game after launching ensuring the customers and their views are listened to.

> *You act as a bridge between the person consuming whatever it is your guys are creating. So if I was working on a game, say I was working on the new F1 game, I'd be the guy who was the voice between the people playing that game and the guys who were making it...*
>
> *-Tom Champion*
> *Community Manager, Eurogamer.net*

Retail:

The final piece of the puzzle the guys who sell the games and hardware to you.

So far we've covered how a game is made and hopefully I've shown you a little about their daily lives. We should now consider other elements of their working life. There are many articles regarding the hours worked in the industry and what is called crunch. This is usually when a game is nearing completion or an important milestone, what happens is a final push to get the game completed and released on time with the highest possible quality bar. To do this companies require their staff to work much longer hours to achieve the highest quality product they can deliver. This can easily be 10-14 hour days and weekends, a lot of the time there will be little or no reimbursement for your efforts. You may get paid, but more likely they will reimburse you with food and time off for the extra time worked, sometimes known as TOIL. I personally have done 3 days and 2 nights without leaving the office and regularly 24hr shifts. Crunch is without a doubt the number one reason people leave the games industry. However if you're willing to pull out all the stops and make every sacrifice you can for the sake of the game, then crunch can also be a fun, rewarding time which could make the difference between a temp and a permanent contract. To aid you during your first period of crunch I've compiled some helpful tips for survival.

Tips for surviving crunch:

Get plenty of rest as and when you can.

Certain departments rely on others to complete their work before they can begin. If you find yourself waiting for work to come in try to rest a bit so you can focus better when it does arrive.

> *Avoid smoking and drinking. Enjoy your coffee and tea, but too much caffeine will make you twitch, try to relax whenever you can as your body needs the small bits of downtime required.*
>
> *- Nelson de Gouveia*
> *Lead Tester, IdeaWorks 3D*

Keep your energy levels high.

With such long hours you will begin to run low on energy, keeping an energy drink or snack around your desk to perk you up is never a bad idea.

Enjoy it.

It's a hard time for everyone involved, but if you can just try to enjoy it, everyone will get along a lot better. Having a fun enjoyable experience rather than one where people are complaining the whole time is an obvious choice. Telling a joke or having a laugh isn't frowned upon as it's good for everyone involved.

> *If you're married or have a partner, having their support and understanding is vital. Crunch can sometimes mean that you don't get to see your wife and kids at all during the week. This can put a huge strain of life outside of work, so their support is essential. Also, having an understanding employer is important. If you're struggling with overtime and need a break, speak to you line-manager about it and see what can be done. Don't just sit there and burn yourself out.*
>
> *-Peter Clark*
> *VFX Artist, Codemasters*

Work as a team.

Share responsibility and work together, it's a team effort so make sure everyone is doing what they can. The day will go quicker, a lot more will be done and less will need doing. Working as an efficient team improves crunch for us all.

Freshen up.

12 hours at a desk in front of a computer, T.V. and development kit isn't pleasant. If you need to, go grab some fresh air, wash your face and generally freshen up a bit. It makes things a bit more bearable.

> *Remember your family comes first. No one ever had "Wish I'd stayed at the office longer" written on their tombstone. Get sleep when you can and try REALLY hard to stay away from the awful snacks they will bring in!*
>
> *- Sherri Graner Ray*
> *Design Director, Schell Games*

Hopefully these tips will aid you through your first crunch period, remember no matter what happens if you need a break make sure you take one. It seems appropriate that as we're discussing the working life of a games developer, we should look at another major issue facing the industry today, the gender divide and what impact this has on all of us within the industry...

So what am I talking about when I mention the gender divide? Quite simply we have an industry which is male dominated, this has always been the case and impacts on you no matter what gender group you belong to. We're dealing with an industry that has for a long time not even considered women as customers. Until the Sims was released, large number of female gamers was unheard of. In recent times organisations have begun to help women in the industry and to champion them and their abilities. These groups help promote women in the industry running conferences and various events each year. I spoke to all of my interviewees and asked them if they thought women face challenges in the industry due to the gender makeup of the industry and whether they thought attitudes were changing. The views varied greatly as you might expect and you can see what they said for themselves later in this book. For my part I have never seen a company not dominated by men and for good or for bad anyone joining the industry needs to recognise that for now they will be joining a predominately male environment.

> *Gaming is no longer just a boy's toy – everyone plays games these days. In testing I have worked with a lot of women and there's no discrimination that I can see. Your promotion and job prospects don't hinge on what sex you are, but on what you can offer the company as an employee.*
>
> *- Marc Robinson*
> *Lead Tester, Capcom*

We've already covered a lot in this chapter about how the industry works, but before we move on we should briefly look at the recent change in education provided for people hoping to join the industry and what additional options it offers you. Until recently you could only study programming. Game courses in Art, Design and even Test have recently begun to be offered up and down the country. Education will never replace experience in terms of what you will learn, but should be considered none the less as a possible aid to getting you into the industry. It might be just what you need to give you the edge over the competition.

Chapter 5: The seal of quality

I want to spend a bit of time discussing Quality Assurance. It is after all where I've spent my time in the industry and has always been seen as a route into the industry, often being overlooked as a career path in itself. I landed my first role testing games in 1999 helping a small publisher get their Christmas releases out on time. I couldn't believe my luck, to actually get paid to play a game seemed like heaven. When I started work I was highly critical, admittedly this was the first piece of early code I had ever seen, but everything I did seemed to lead to a bug and every single one of them went into the database. On my third day, the manager and a lead took me aside and told me I was entering more than three times the amount of bugs than the other testers and that I should keep it up and since then I always have. Being highly critical has always done me well in my career. After all if you are hired to ensure the best possible quality of a product, then why would you strive for anything else? As time progresses you start to realise that sometimes you don't always need to be so critical. You begin to identify where and when it's best for the title to undergo certain types of tests and how to deploy these effectively.

In this chapter we'll look at the work a Q.A. department does, how this affects the other teams, where Q.A. can lead you on your career and why it's still the best place to start, no matter what you want to end up doing.

> *I'd never in a million years think about approaching the start of a game development without fundamentally thinking about where Q.A. are going to contribute to it and exactly what ways we can get them to be more involved, because they are so valuable.*
>
> *- Andrew Shenton*
> *Technical Manager, Blitz Games*

As the name suggests Q.A. is employed to provide Quality Assurance, i.e. that the team attempts to make the game as good as it can possibly be. This can take a variety of forms from functional testing, standards preparation and testing, localising the game into other languages, organising focus tests or public Beta tests through to purely giving their thoughts on new additions to the game. The primary role of the test department is functional testing, which is to look for problems in the game and report these to the development team who then attempt to fix the problem. Now these problems can literally be anything that looks, sounds or feels wrong. Anyone can find an obvious problem, it's the hidden, hard to reach problems that a skilled tester will report. The chart below shows what happens once a bug is found and how these bugs are handled internally:

The bug lifecycle:

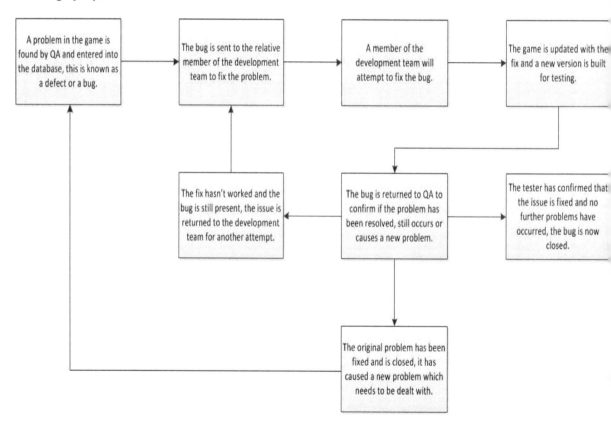

Due to the nature of development the Q.A. team could be physically located away from the development team for a variety of reasons. Because the team may be in a different part of the building, offsite or even in another building all together a tester needs to be able to communicate clearly and concisely on each and every bug they enter into the database. No matter what department you work in, you will come across and deal with bugs so it's important that anyone can read a bug, understand how to view the problem and how serious that problem may be. Let's have a look at a how a bug is written and why.

> Q.A. is a great first stepping stone to get into the industry, as you get a taste of how both developers and publishers work and from there you can decide where you want to take your career.
>
> -Sophie Blackmore
> Senior Designer, Rockstar Games

A typical bug report will normally contain video or images to help the developer find the problem:

Level 6: Fails to continue after the 2nd cut-scene

Severity: A

The user has found that level 6 fails to continue after the 2nd cut-scene, once the scene finishes that game fails to return to the level and play cannot continue.

Steps to reproduce:

1) Load the game
2) Play through until level 6
3) Play level 6 until the 2nd cut-scene
4) Observe when the cut-scene ends the game does not return to the level

Reproduced: 3/3

Expected results: The game continues as normal

As you can see above a bug consists of the following

- A title/summary
- A detailed report
- Steps to reproduce
- A reproduction rate
- Expected Results
- Severity

A title or summary:
This should (in a couple of words) explain the problem.

A detailed report:
A short account of the nature of the bug, what occurs, where and what was happening at the time. This needs to be short, clear and, most importantly, convey all the information correctly so that the department who will fix the bug have a complete understanding as to its nature. Although short, it should contain all details without changing subject or including superfluous information.

Steps to reproduce:
This is a step by step guide on how to recreate the bug so anyone can pick up the bug and the software and get the bug to occur by following your steps.

A reproduction rate:
How often does the bug occur? Developers need to know this to know how long they should spend trying to repeat the bug. If a developer cannot repeat the bug they are unlikely to be able to fix it.

Expected results:
This isn't always needed, but it often helps to tell the department what you would expect to happen instead of the bug occurring.

Severity:
How serious is the issue? This is recorded in grades usually of A, B and C as an identifier to how serious the problem is. A being for problems that cannot be allowed in the release like crashes, B is used for problems which although serious they are not quite as serious as A class problems, things like a missing bit of speech or a function

not working would fall into this category. The C category is used for minor problems like small graphical errors or the wrong spelling of text.

With a well written bug you should aim to include all of the above with just the right level of detail, here are a few more bug writing tips for the budding tester.

Do not offend! Many people have worked long and hard to get the game to the state it's in. Always make sure that your bug is objective and does not contain personal views using words like "crap" or "rubbish" is never acceptable and will only cause offence.

There will be times when you find a subjective bug, something that you feel is a bug but other people may feel isn't a bug. Always discuss with your colleagues and lead before entering such bugs, as others may not feel the same about the issue. Please note that these issues usually occur when balancing the game.

Always use a spell checker and always reread your bug to make sure it makes sense. A tester must be clear with each and every bug as they often communicate over great distances and anything to improve efficiency in tackling a bug is always welcome.

Any tester who remembers the simple advice above will do well in Quality Assurance. Functional testing (the main bulk of Q.A. work) is usually split into two formats, destructive testing and test plans. Destructive testing gives a tester the opportunity to use their imagination and skill as a tester to break the game anyway they choose. Test plans are something anyone in any department should consider so let's look at them in more detail.

The aim of the test plan is to ensure that all of the main parts of the game are tested and checked on a regular basis. To this end, it is essential that you identify the main areas of the game that you want checked on a regular basis. You cannot cover for every eventuality in a test plan; it is unrealistic to think that you can. All you can do is provide a guide to the areas that need checking and allow your test-team to follow this guide, applying their own tests and experience to the task. This allows leads and management to actively track what has been tested and what is remaining on each version/build that Q.A. receives. The test plan has many uses, as aside from giving Q.A. some testing structure, it can be used to identify how quickly Q.A. turn around a build, while ensuring important features are covered throughout the test cycle. A typical test plan will cover essential aspects of the game like level progression and unlocks whilst also pointing out different features to the tester and prompting them on possible ways of breaking these. Everyone should ensure that they check the test plan contains the important elements they need regularly tested. A test plan should never be the entirety of your testing, it should be balanced with free form destructive testing.

A test-plan will only really be in use from Alpha onwards when the game contains all of the levels/sections. Up until this time, the test-cycles will be flexible and varied to meet demand. The Lead Tester will be responsible for agreeing these test-cycles with the Producer of each project and creating the test plan itself. A full test cycle from Alpha onwards would ideally last no longer than 2-3 days in all. This obviously can vary depending on the size of the test team and product, but it is a good thing to aim for. The test cycle would typically take in:

- Regression of bugs marked as fixed in the database
- One cycle of the test plan
- Playthroughs on all difficulties, of all levels

A typical test plan should be broken down into 2 sections:

- The Front Page, where the overall progress can be checked and tasks assigned.
- The Level/Area, where the actual test instructions for a level are laid out and all results and comments are recorded by the tester.

To create a test plan we need to start by assessing the game, either manually or by checking the design documents. See how many levels there are, if it is single player, co-op, multiplayer, if there are varying levels of difficulty?

You should now try breaking down the game into manageable chunks (such as levels), identify the prevailing characteristics and features of the game. Generally, a game can be broken down into the following test groups, but of course games vary wildly so this cannot be used as a rule.

Single Player

- Visual
- Audio
- Boundary Checking

- A.I.
- Camera
- Options
- Cut-scenes
- Area/level specific events (progression)
- Objects/Scenery
- Miscellaneous

Multiplayer

- No. of players
- No. of maps
- No. of options

Front End & Pause menu

- Options
- Load & Save
- Button Mapping

Other

- Soak Tests
- Playthroughs
- Achievements
- Unlocks

The key to a successful test plan is to ensure that all main areas of the game are covered by your test team on a regular basis. You can only guide your team towards the areas of the game you want tested and allow their testing skills and application to find the problems with the game. To this end, you should take an overall look at the game and identify the parts/features that are prevalent throughout and create a basic list of questions and checks that ensures the tester will check them all for each and every level. This will be your template for each level. Then you should look at the levels and identify the parts that are individual to each level and compose a set of tests for each level that cover these. Once this is done, the main level-by-level single player content of your test-plan should be identified.

As you can see a good test plan is important in targeting areas of the game and ensuring the game is ready for release. It's almost a bible for the final phase of creating the game. With our knowledge of this and functional testing we should have a look at some of the other functions a Q.A. department may have...

Localisation

Localisation is when the game is translated to a different language, commonly this is French, Italian, German and Spanish (but could include any language whatsoever). This type of testing is usually split into two groups, functional checks and translated checks:

Translated checks is translating the text and confirming the translation makes sense in the new language.

Functional checks are to confirm the text is legible, fits on screen and does not collide with other text or text borders.

Focus testing

As we mentioned earlier a focus test is when the public play the game and give us their opinions. Usually Q.A. would support any focus test in a variety of ways by confirming the game is in a playable state for the test and ensuring that any results are handled correctly, some of which will be tasks for people whilst others will be bugs. While production is likely to handle the tasks, Q.A. is of course responsible for any bugs.

Beta testing

If a game is released as a Beta test, a method of handling any problems reported and working out feedback from actual bugs is needed. Q.A. is in an ideal position to process these problems and ensure that the Beta test is an asset to the games development.

Load testing

A load test is when the game's servers are tested to see if they can handle a lot of traffic. This simulation is conducted by Q.A. to ensure that on release the game does not suffer from latency issues.

Demo testing

When a demo or a review version of the game is required, it is of course tested before being used. This ensures that the game will be reflected in a good light to the end user.

Manual checking

The games manual is usually checked by the Q.A. team to ensure the language, punctuation, translation and content are all correct and free from any mistakes.

Quality feedback

When a new feature is added to a game, the person responsible may come down to Q.A. to discuss if the feature is an improvement or something which doesn't enhance the experience. This type of qualitative feedback will often ensure a better product after Q.A. Testers are normally very passionate and clued up to the industry at large and gaming in general.

Balancing the game

One of the hardest parts of game creation is working out the difficulty curve as you don't want the game to be too hard or too easy. You don't want a level to be hard and then followed by an easy level. You certainly don't want a game to be too hard for a player to complete nor too easy. So getting the ideal difficulty curve can be quite a challenge, ideally you want a game to start off easy and get gradually harder as it progresses without any peaks or troughs in this.

The way a game is balanced is often critical to its success. An ideal game balance is shown below:

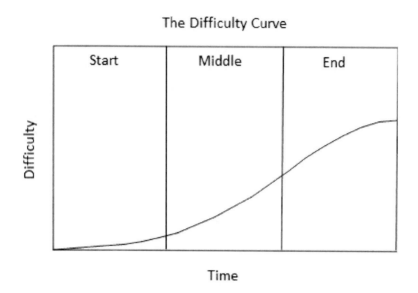

The Difficulty Curve

As you can imagine different people have different skills at different games, so it's important that any balancing work involves a wide range of people. As you can see game balancing is important and tricky to perfect.

Smoke testing

A smoke test is a quick test, usually just to confirm each level in a game loads. This test is carried out to ensure a new version is ready for the test team. If the majority of levels don't load than Q.A. will not use that build, but wait for a fixed version to arrive.

Submission testing

Submission testing is very important to any console game and therefore a tester with a decent amount of submission knowledge is an asset to any developer.

Now we know the type of work a Q.A. department deals with, we should look at why Q.A. is a great place to start and learn about the industry. Because of the nature of Q.A., the team will directly affect each and every person's work load. A normal bug database will contain thousands of bugs which need to be fixed prior to release. This means every coder, artist, animator, designer and audio member working on the project will get work from Q.A. This can be quite demoralising because the bulk of these bugs come at the end of a project when people really start to wish for it to end. This means the team can become quite demoralised, an artist friend of mine once told me it took him years to understand that Q.A. were not criticising his work, but actually getting him to improve and enhance his work. It also means that a good Q.A. tester will take great care when writing bugs, always avoiding terms which may annoy a team member. This also means that test will come into contact with every department in the studio and coupled with the fact that Q.A. deals with the game from start to finish, it means it's the best place for any junior in the industry to begin. You get to see how the game is made from start to finish and you get to discuss problems with everyone. This means you have great opportunities to learn about various careers in the industry and what they might lead to, how much you might earn and what it might take to get there. This opportunity to learn is one that anyone interested in games careers should aim for. Q.A. has always been seen as a gateway to the industry so let's look at some of the paths a tester might move onto and why Q.A. is an asset for these departments.

Production

Producers deal with every single team on the project daily and a good producer can understand and relate to each department's day and needs on a project. Any producer who has spent time in Q.A. will have this knowledge and understanding, as well as a good relationship with members of these departments. A large part of a producer's role is scheduling and any Q.A. lead or manager will have experience of scheduling builds and teams within their department. These factors mean that an experienced Q.A. tester will be an asset to any production team.

Design

Testers love games, they test them all day and probably play them whenever they can. They usually have a large collection of games and a huge passion for the industry, a decent tester will always be thinking about the user interface and the users experience throughout the game. This way of thinking and the knowledge of the market are great skills for the design team and due to this, designers often come from Q.A. This means that junior design roles are rarely advertised as when they come up the ideal candidate is usually to be found in Q.A.

Every other department

Because testers deal with every department, it gives junior members the opportunity to network and learn. This means when any junior role which comes up may well be filled by a member of Q.A. I've seen good testers going to every possible role from production to code, community management to art and animation. If the tester is hard working and a junior role comes up, then the fit is usually ideal.

One thing I would like to add when considering the potential roles Q.A. may lead to is to consider and weigh up the potential of a career in Q.A. itself. Often an overlooked career path you usually find that by their 5th year a tester has left Q.A., either for a role in another department or for a different career entirely. It's quite rare to find testers with over ten years experience. This means that someone who has a lot of Q.A. experience can be highly respected and in demand when it comes to vacancies. A Q.A. manager has the responsibility for quality and ensuring that this is of a high standard for every title a studio produces which is not only something to be proud of, but also something that ensures the games industry will continue to thrive and entertain for years to come. No one will ever doubt that a career in Q.A. is a hard and often ignored career path in the industry, but it is one and one that you can be proud of.

Chapter 6: Credits

In this chapter we have the original interviews conducted with industry professionals as research for this book. I hope these will give you an insight into the various roles and challenges that these professionals deal with every day. Throughout the course of writing this book I have been knocked out by the kind generosity of all of those who agreed to be interviewed. With some old friends it was nice to catch up and see how far they had come and I thoroughly enjoyed meeting new professionals who go through the similar trials, pain and joy we all do in the industry. These lovely people gave vastly different opinions and advice, even after a decade thinking I had seen it all some of the answers genuinely came as a surprise to me. I hope you enjoy reading these interviews as much as I did conducting and collecting them, but most of all I hope it helps you understand the career path you want to take and get there fully aware of how hard game creation can actually be. Finally I have to point out that the opinions and views mentioned during these interviews are those of the individual and do not in any way shape or form represent the companies they work for.

You can find the following interviews in this section:

- Daniel Lodge, Lead Artist for Doublesix Games
- Peter Clark, VFX Artist for Codemasters
- Nathan McCree, Audio Director for Vatra Games
- Andrew Smith, Director for Split Milk Studios
- Rhys Twelves, Lead Programmer for Bioware
- Barry Northern, Senior Game Developer for 4T2 Entertainment
- Sherri Graner Ray, Design Director for Schell Games
- Sophie Blackmore, Senior Designer for Rockstar Games
- Will Luton, Creative Director for Mobile Pie
- Jez Harris, Production Manager for Supermassive Games
- Aaron Yeung, Associate Producer for Doublesix Games
- Paul Sedgmore, Q.A. Manager for Colossal Games
- Nick Scurr, Senior Tester for FreeStyleGames
- Nelson de Gouveia, Lead Tester for IdeaWorks 3D
- Marc Robinson, Q.A. Tester for Capcom
- Leo Tan, Senior P.R. Manager for Capcom
- Tom Champion, Community Manager for Eurogamer.net
- Dan Pearson, Senior Staff Writer for Gamesindustry.biz
- James Grant, H.R. Services Manager for Gamesindustry.biz

- Bill Stone, Self-employed Independent retailer
- Eamonn Mgherbi, Managing Director for Avatar Games Recruitment

Name:	Daniel Lodge	*Currently working for:*	Doublesix Games
Age:	25	*Current role:*	Lead Artist
Sex:	Male	*Length of Service:*	3 years

I met Dan through a friend of mine we started by looking at his career so far.
Why did you want to get into the games industry?

I feel many of the games I play aren't creative enough as they cater for the lowest common denominator. Some of the "big" games that we play today are insultingly dull and cliché in my opinion. I hoped and continue to aspire to give gamers some credit, to help video games mature as a medium and to create games that have artistic and intellectual merit. I want to provide games for those guys who want more than another fantasy RPG or "realistic" FPS.

How long have you worked in the industry?

I did three months as a Q.A. Tester at Traveller's Tales before starting as a Junior Artist at Doublesix Games where we specialise in digital download games such as Burn Zombie Burn! and All Zombies Must Die. I've been at Doublesix for over three years now and have climbed the ranks to Lead Artist where I am currently responsible for the art on the new, multi-platform IP, Strike Suit Zero.

So you left a more traditional developer (console games) for one that uses digital download. Do you feel downloading games has an advantage?"

Well actually the bulk of what we do is for consoles (XBLA and PlayStation Home). We also publish our games for P.C. through Steam. We have done some iPhone stuff in the past (Babeorella, Iron-Man Aerial Assault), but that isn't our focus. I think digital download is great for everyone, the market will only grow. As developers, digital distribution allows us to cut out the expensive and risky business of manufacturing, storing and distributing hard copies of our games, this means we are less reliant on huge publishers and subsequently their sometimes difficult requests. We get more ownership of our work. It also goes some way to de-risking innovation. For gamers, the platform provides cheaper games that are often more accessible than large AAA titles. You don't have to invest tens of hours (or pounds) into them to get some enjoyment. I see games like Limbo in the same light as films. I buy them and will sometimes play them through in a single evening. I'm a busy guy so I can really appreciate a short, but high quality experience. I hate games that pad themselves out with repetition to make it seem like they are better value. Of course there are negatives to working on digital download titles too. Our budgets are smaller so there is less time for pre-production and getting stuff wrong. We don't always have amazing tools or engines to play with, but the consumer won't look on our work any differently for it. Our stuff is compared to the big boys who have many times our budgets and timescales. Whilst I put these things down as negatives, some of us can turn that around and enjoy the challenge of it all.

Who have you worked for in the industry?

Traveller's Tales, Kuju Surrey, Doublesix Games

What do you do in the industry?

Currently I lead a 5/6 man art team on Strike Suit Zero. My responsibilities include the planning and management of the art aspects of the project in collaboration with our producer. I manage the art style of the game and work closely with the individual members of my team to ensure they are working efficiently, that they are on style and the quality of work is maintained for all art going in game. I liaise with my Lead Coder and Lead Designer to ensure their art requirements are met and, when I can tear myself away from meetings, I contribute to the game's art directly, usually in a fairly strategic fashion.

If I was an applicant would it be better for my show reel to conform to the studios style or is it better to show off my own work?

I think the answer to that would vary from studio to studio. At Doublesix we don't have a "house style" so I look for flexible artists. Guys with traditional skills that will allow them to quickly adapt to any style we need them to work to. Having something in your portfolio that relates to what we have done in the past is definitely a good move though, it shows you could have done what would have been asked of you, but I'd be concerned if I only saw realistic work or I only saw stylized work. Like I say though, my opinion is definitely not universal. I've met Art Directors in the past that have a hard time judging useful skills from anything but directly relevant work. Their loss!

What would you say is the highlight of your career so far?

The day my first game released (South Park Let's Go Tower Defence Play) and I sat down to play it at home with my girl friend, my little brother and his house-mate. The three of them are all big South Park fans. We got some beers in and played it all night. They genuinely loved the game. Seeing them enjoy all the hard work we put in was great. None of us could believe it. I had started my career!

So what would you consider the lowlight of your career so far?

I recently had to put someone through a competency review. I've worked with the guy for over a year and we have become friends. It was horrible having to tell this guy who loves what he does that he has to improve his performance or risk losing his position at the studio. Also, it doesn't happen that often, but I hate it when there is bigotry between the disciplines. We are all professionals so we should treat each other with equal respect. I don't like the generalisations that get thrown about sometimes, they are not positive.

Do you think there's a lot of infighting (between the disciplines) when making a game? After all with so many creative people opinions will vary greatly.

Generally no, I try hard to play down the seams between the disciplines and at Doublesix the rapport between the guys is healthy. Occasionally comments will be made but we resolve them quickly. I don't think it's fair to generalise. You will sometimes come across the (inaccurate) stereotype that artists break everything, that they don't care about efficiency and that the coders need to baby sit them. Of course you will come across artists who can be described like that, but in turn I know a lot of artists who are very intelligent about the way they work and who would find this stereotype patronising and offensive. It's a natural tribal thing that we see in all aspects of life, but when we lump people into categories and start arguing over which discipline is more necessary than the next, we risk losing access to valuable skills. Whether it's a designer with aesthetic flair or a coder with great ideas for game play, it makes sense to benefit from their input. Of all the disciplines, the guys who get it roughest, in my experience, are producers. If you aspire to work as a producer, my advice to you is, integrate with the team, always remember you are there to facilitate development, to help solve problems. You are not there to swing your ego around and snatch all the credit. You need to listen and learn and treat people with respect. If you help solve problems you will always be welcome on any dev. team worth its salt.

How did you originally get into the industry and did you do anything unique to increase your chances?

My dad used to bring home computers from work and so I had access to computer games much earlier than my many of my friends. Both my brothers would play games relentlessly and whilst I played a lot too, I used to criticise them for their idle life styles since I liked to be more active and to create stuff. When I got older I started to see the potential of games as a medium. I like to analyse everything around me and so naturally had lots opinions about how I thought games should be. That's when I got into modding from a project management angle. I soon learnt that mods. only progress when you have a dedicated core team of skilled people regularly contributing. In frustration I began to contribute "real" work to my mod. project as a texture artist and graphic designer as well as game design and project management. At that point I was preparing to go to study at university. I ended up studying Graphic Communication at the Fareham campus at UCA. I'd heard bad things about games degrees and felt I needed a core skill, something that would be transferable if I decided to change career direction. I think it really paid off. I now have some in depth knowledge in graphic design which I use daily. I have a different way of seeing things to the guys with fine art or animation backgrounds. During my second year I organised work experience at Kuju Surrey where I met my future Art Director at Doublesix. I went on to do another unpaid work placement just as Doublesix formed. Those placements allowed me to make an impression on some artists who would later be in a position to hire me. Of course for an artist it's all about a high quality and relevant portfolio though.

How did you get into your current role?

For the first two years of my career I worked in a team that apart from me was made up exclusively of senior artists. A lot of responsibility was placed on me from day one. My lead went on a holiday with his family during my first submission as an artist, I felt responsible for our project three months into the job. As some of the senior guys left, they were replaced with junior artists. Despite Doublesix having a small art team we tend to make up to three games simultaneously. With the number of available senior artists limited an opportunity arose for me to lead the SSZ team. I'd been vocal about the project and I'd previously made a good impression on the code team as a fairly technical artist. I guess I just had a lot of backing from the team so management decided to take a risk and give me the project. I like to think it's paying off, look out for Strike Suit Zero and see what you think yourselves.

What advice would you give to people looking to be a lead artist in the industry?

Practice as much as you can, work and rework pieces. Always finish what you start as there is a lot to learn in the final stages of a piece. Don't under estimate traditional skills, you will need to be able to draw on art fundamentals, drawing, painting, colour, composition, lighting theory. Never look at any task as "just a crate, just a chair, just a generic civilian" everything should tell a story. I think that's the difference between a technician and an artist.

If hiring, would you put more emphasis on education or experience?

After several rounds of interviewing and hiring people I would say I have learnt the value of candidates with higher education. Higher education within art and design helps an individual develop their analytic skills as well as some context within art at the broader spectrum. These things aid in problem solving and seeing further than a technician's aim of just coldly aspiring to realism. I look to hire artists who can identify and reproduce the most evocative aspects of reality before considering how they could be stylised if appropriate.

So would you dismiss an artist with no education but a high quality show reel?

I would never dismiss a high quality show reel. If I interview a candidate with no formal higher education in art or design I just amend the way I conduct the interview. They need to assure me that they have some depth and understanding to what they are doing. That they have some contextual understanding and that they will grow. I've come across situations where candidates have essentially learnt a few tricks which they use to great effect, but when they are unable to use those things they have no framework to support them. I think that higher education can help to provide that framework as well as a level of project experience due to the course work based nature of most art and design courses.

Do you have any final thoughts for people hoping to become a lead artist in the games industry?

If you want to rush to the position of lead artist think carefully about it. The managerial responsibilities associated with a lead position can distance you from the art itself and at times it is frustrating. You will start to feel like a producer. Other times you will need solutions to everyone's problems as the team becomes dependant on you for the answers to everything. Any criticism of any visual element of the game weighs on your shoulders. You will face all kinds of challenges to your vision, they are inevitable. If you can handle that and if you like the idea of cooperating with a team of highly skilled professionals to realise their unified vision, then good luck, you are in for a treat!

Would you recommend not climbing the career ladder? Are there more benefits sticking with what you love over the added responsibilities?

I would say it all depends on what you like doing and what you are good at. Some people find themselves leading whenever they are in a team, it's natural to them. You need to have empathy, to want to help people, to fix problems. You need to look at the project as a whole. It's not about abusing your power so you can give yourself the "best" tasks or even necessarily doing the best artwork yourself. You need to utilise your team's skill set effectively, to boil your style down to a rule set and communicate that effectively to your team so they can implement it correctly. I love all that. But I know some artists just want to get their heads down and plough through their task lists. If that's you then you may not enjoy a lead position.

With regards to actually working in the industry, what would you say is the best thing about lead artist?

I'm so grateful for the opportunity to direct the creative energies of a small, but very talented team of artists, to help build something we can all be proud of. I love to create beautiful things and this job allows me to try to do that.

What's the worst thing about lead artist?

Well, there is a lot of expectation placed on me. That in itself is not a problem, I like feeling forced to step up my game all the time, but it can be stressful with so little experience to back me up. I want to make sure the games I work on look the very best they can and that's what keeps me up at night. I keep a notebook by my bed so I can list what I should remember to fix in the morning. It's sort of obsessive I know, but I think you have to invest that kind of passion to get good at what you do.

So what's an average day for a lead artist like?

I'll boot up and make a coffee whilst I wait to log in. Check my emails for anything urgent. Often I will have a meeting booked, sometimes more than one. We may be having a leads meeting where I get together with the other leads to address any issues and keep updated. We might be planning the next short term goals or putting together a plan for addressing external feedback. I might be doing an art review with my art team. Meetings are splattered throughout my usual day. When I'm not in meetings, each artist will come to me for help and advice or to sign off on completed tasks. Sometimes I get members of the code and design teams requesting art support which I deal with or delegate to other artists if necessary. When I'm not in meetings or supporting the team, I get the chance to work on the art tasks assigned to me. This could be anything, but recently it's been a lot of hard surface and environment stuff.

Do you have any tips for surviving crunch?

We have never really crunched that hard at Doublesix. I mean, we do sometimes stay late. The art team and I have been known to put a lot of hours in, but it's always been voluntary and it's more laid back, like hanging out. The company allows us to expense food so we'll get Wagamama's. I'll sometimes get a few beers and put some music on and we stay till last trains or whatever. We just do this periodically when we feel we are getting a bit behind but it's not a big rush at the end. Many of my colleagues are ex EA guys and they tell some horrible stories.

So what are the longest hours you've worked during a crunch?

Is that supposed to be a badge of honour or something? Silly hours I suppose, something like 9 a.m. till 3a.m. As I said though, it was self inflicted "crunch"; I was working from home on the first Strikesuit I modelled.

If you could change one thing about the industry what would that be?

I'd get people to make more games with real depth, beautiful, horrific, euphoric and melancholic games.

Do you feel that the games industry is becoming less creative and more confined to the genres we have created?

You only have to see the numbers suffixing the latest releases to see the extent to which we rely on our own medium's cliché. That said I doubt we are becoming less creative and more confined. The way I see it, gaming is such a huge deal now, it's so big that we really should be seeing more mature games surfacing. Of course I say that while working at a studio that has released two Zombie games in the last three years! I think it will happen, that we will see games do more but the change will be slow. After all, the industry is mostly made up of people who loved the games that came before. It kind of makes sense that they would want to make similar style games.

How do you feel about the challenges women face in the industry?

I honestly think women have it easier than guys as a developer. Women stand out immediately just because they aren't part of the overwhelming majority of male video game professionals. Standing out can be tough so that gives the ladies a leg up. That's not to say women don't have to work hard to get hired. At Doublesix we don't differentiate between men and women in a professional sense so women face no greater challenge than men do. I've worked with several female employees, an artist and an animator; they were both great people to have around. My experience is pretty much strictly development though. I know like most industries it can be tougher at the higher end of management for larger companies. From time to time you see the sort of ridiculous things written about women like Jade Raymond for example.

Do you think attitudes to women are changing in the industry?

Perhaps mildly. As the industry matures attitudes will change. When large amounts of money are concerned I think people start to care less about the gender of their employees and more about their profits. I would be surprised if the gender of a work force and profits are linked and if that is the case then I expect equality should follow.

Do you feel women need to work harder to prove themselves in the industry?

As in any industry there will be sexism. I've never come across the classic kind of sexism you might assume (baring one particular calendar). If anything I've only seen the advantages of being a women working in games. Like I said before, you stand out and if you're good then that can only be a positive thing.

If you could offer one piece of advice to someone starting out in the industry what would that be?

Don't wait for anyone else. Have a long, hard think then start making games and never stop. Do those things and you can't fail! Good luck!

Thanks for your time Dan. It's been a pleasure meeting you.

Name:	Peter Clark	Currently working for:	Codemasters
Age:	33	Current role:	VFX Artist
Sex:	Male	Length of Service:	5 years

Pete and I used to work together in Scotland at Vis Entertainment. He's a talented VFX artist with several years experience. It was good to find out what he had been up to since we last worked together.

Why did you want to get into the games industry?

To be honest, I didn't. I was studying to be Animator at university and had dreams of working for Disney/Pixar. However, if I'm brutally honest, I needed a job after graduating and I was lucky enough to find one in the games industry. I've been in the industry ever since.

How long have you worked in the industry?

11 years

Who have you worked for in the industry?

VIS Entertainment, DC Studios, Firebrand Games, Cohort Studios and Codemasters

What do you do in the industry?

Currently I'm Senior VFX Artist at Codemasters, but over the course of my career I have working in nearly all aspects of Art including Lead Environment Artist, Senior Vehicle Artist, Character Artist, Animator, Technical Artist and Concept

That's quite a lot of roles in the Art Department. Could you explain the differences between them?

As Lead Environment Artist, I was responsible for the environment art team and the visual look of the levels. I'd liaise with the concept artists and try to capture their vision of an environment in 3D space. I'd brief the other environment artists on work required and conduct reviews of each level during production.

As Senior Vehicle Artist, I was responsible for creating vehicles of the game as well as offering support and mentoring the other artists in the group.

As Character Artist, I was responsible for the concepting and creating of character models and textures of use in the game. I'd work closely with the animators during development to ensure the models met the requirements of the animators with regard to anatomy and joint limitations.

As an Animator, I was responsible for creating all animated sequences for the game. As I was an animator of a sprite based game, my animation work was 2D sprite based animations, which included a range of images that are then played in order to create the animated sequence.

As Technical Artist, I was responsible for 'bridging the gap' between Artists and Programmers. I worked closely with the Lead Artist and Lead Programmer to ensure that all pipeline and workflows were smooth. I was also responsible for creating any tools that the artists required to ease their workflow and increase productivity. Other tasks included creating MEL scripts, shaders, lighting and offing technical support for artists as well as ensuring that all art assets meet the technical specifications of the game and fit within budget.

As Senior VFX artist, I am responsible for creating all particle based Visual Effects for the game such as explosions, muzzle flashes, ambient environment effects, screen effects, dust kickup for car wheels etc. I am also responsible for the planning of all VFX for the game and ensuring that all tasks are delivered on time and to a high standard. I also offer support and mentoring for the other VFX artists.

As Concept Artist, I was responsible for concepting the look of the game and in-game assets such as props and characters. The Concept Artist works closely with the Art Director in creating the artistic style and feel of a game.

What would you say is the highlight of your career so far?

Landing a job at Codemasters! I've been a fan of Codemasters games ever since the early TOCA and Colin McRae Rally games. I'm a huge Motorsport and Racing fan, so being able to work on titles such as Dirt3 and F1 2011 really is a highlight for me.

I remember you were always interested in racing when we worked together, do you feel that it's important to try to work on the type of games you love?

For me it was, but it really does depend on the individual. I know many developers who don't wish to work on their favourite games and genres as they don't want to lose interest in those games. Personally, I like working in all areas of the games industry, however, working on some of my favourite games and being able to influence and contribute towards their success is very rewarding indeed.

So what would you consider the lowlight of your career so far?

Redundancy is an unfortunate and all too common aspect of the Games Industry it seems. It's especially harder now that I am a family man with 2 children. After being made redundant from Cohort Studios, there were very little opportunities in Scotland that appealed to me, so we made the decision to sell our house and move down to England so I could work for Codemasters. This meant I could work on the games I love, but at the cost of my wife's job, her friends, my friends and our children's friends. Not to mention the move away from family and our support network. Being made redundant isn't just a case of losing your job, sometimes you lose much, much more.

We actually worked for two companies that both went bankrupt on us. Do you feel that instability is a common part of the industry?

Unfortunately, it seems that way. Over the past few years we have seen not only small studios, but some of the industry greats closing down and shutting up shop. It seems that unless you make a hit title these days, the studios struggle to remain open. Due to the production costs of games, many studios are unable to continue production if they simply don't make a profit, resulting in closure. Tax breaks and other incentives could potentially help alleviate some of those costs and give studios more of a fighting chance in a very competitive industry.

How did you originally get into the industry and did you do anything unique to increase your chances?

This is an interesting question with a somewhat funny answer. Simply put, I got into the industry as a result of a prank by my flat-mate. I received a phone call from my flat-mate early one morning saying that an Art Director from a games studio was at the college and he'd seen my work and wanted to speak to me. Delighted, I grabbed my portfolio and ran down to the college. The Art Director was indeed at the college, so I approached him and introduced myself. He informed me that he wasn't there to see me after all, but there were others he wanted to speak to. My flat-mate had stitched me up. Fortunately for me, the Art Director said he did have a spare few minutes if I was willing to show him my work, so I jumped at the chance. He offered me an interview the following week along with the other 5 students he had seen. I was the only one to get the job. So truth be told, I got into the industry because of a prank and some good fortune.

How did you get into your current role?

I was the Technical Artist at Cohort Studios. Quite early on in the development of The Shoot, it became apparent we'd need a lot of particle FX. At that time, Cohort didn't have a VFX artist, so it was decided that I was the best suited person for the job. I was reluctant at first as VFX wasn't an area I'd done before, at that time, I was more interested in the technical side of artwork...little did I know then about how technical Visual Effects work is. I was allowed to continue doing Technical Art as well as VFX work, so this suited me well. VFX seemed to come quite naturally to me. Very quickly I became heavily involved in creating VFX and then helping design the particle engine. I haven't looked back since.

What advice would you give to people looking to be a VFX Artist in the industry?

Reference gathering, study movies and game VFX. Look at videos of explosions, how fire moves, how snow falls. A lot of VFX work is in the timing of things. So many explosions lack the 'force' in the effect. Through studying the dynamics of an explosion, you can get a real sense of force into your work. Also look at working with particles in software such as Maya, 3DS Max, Houdini, Fume FX and Particle Illusion. I also like to draw my Visual Effects. This might seem strange as a lot of VFX work is about movement, but I find that drawing an explosion, for example, gives me a great sense of what is happening within that explosion, how the debris flies out and then falls. How the smoke billows, the shape and movement of a fireball. Once you have a good understanding of what it is you're trying to create and how they should look, everything becomes much easier.

You're actually saying that we should study explosions, quite a fun suggestion. Do you attempt to make VFX as realistic as possible or is it game dependant?

It really is dependent on the style of game. For Operation Flashpoint, we looked to create an authentic experience. This doesn't necessarily mean 'realistic', therefore a lot of our explosions looked a little more impressive that they do in reality. In real life, explosions are quite boring. All you really see in a large dust plume and lots of debris. It's really only in Hollywood that you see the massive fireballs and burning embers and flying sparks etc. Hollywood makes explosions look cool.... and we try to do the same. On the other hand, if you're working on a cartoony based game, then a realistic/authentic explosion or smoke plume would look somewhat out of place, so the effects really need to be balanced to the art direction and style of each game. This is a great challenge for VFX artists (and all artists alike) as they need to be able to use their knowledge and skills and adapt them to multiple situations and artistic styles from project to project.

If hiring would you put more emphasis on education or experience?

I'd say experience. While I am all for new blood getting into the industry, I feel that you can't beat experience. Someone who has worked on multiple titles and has been around the industry for many years is invaluable. Talent also plays a huge part as well. However, if I had two portfolios of artwork in front of me, one from an artist with a University Degree and one with no formal qualifications, I'd still look at the artist quality of the work over academic achievement.

Do you have any final thoughts for people hoping to become a VFX Artist in the games industry?

Research what part of the Industry you wish to get into. A VFX artist who is only interested in explosions and bullet impacts won't really get much satisfaction from working on, say, a racing title. That being said, a VFX artist should be able to change and adapt their skills regardless of style, genre or direction of a game.

With regards to actually working in the industry, what would you say is the best thing about VFX artist?

The best thing about my role is I get to blow s**t up! I get to create effects that can make the player sit up and say "Wow! Did you just see that explosion!" or "That was an awesome crash! Did you see the pieces go flying?" Visual Effects is exactly what is says... Visual! It's one of the areas of game development that if done well, can bring a level or game to life. Look at KillZone 3... Now imagine it without all the ambient effects, dust, embers, sparks and explosions. Many people go to the movies and say "The special effects were awesome!" that's what I want people to say about the games I work on.

What's the worst thing about VFX artist?

Technical limitations, lack of understanding and a shortfall in talented VFX artists. Visual effects in games are years away from being able to create the same quality of effects that Hollywood can bring, due to the limitations of what can be done on consoles and PC's..... We'll get there though. I also find that VFX seem to be placed quite low in terms of priority when developing a lot of games. This is probably due to a lack of understanding about what is achievable with VFX and how much they can add to a game. Regardless of what game it is you're making, a good VFX artist can change the mood of a scene with just one effect. A shortfall in talented VFX artists within the games industry is also a challenge. Trying to find someone with the necessary skills can sometimes take a very long time. Again, this can possibly be linked to a lack of understanding about game VFX. Many artists thinking of getting into the industry think of Environment Art, Characters or Concept but few probably think about Visual Effects.

So what's an average day for a VFX Artist like?

I'll get a brief or an idea presented to me about a specific effect. We'll go though that idea and talk about things such as colour, speed, timing, size, volume etc. I'll then start to gather some reference material together such as videos or pictures. Sometimes I'll even film a specific 'effect' myself, such as rainfall or a puddle splash. Once I have all the relevant information and reference required, I'll start to block out the effect using the particle editor. I'll usually just use flat colours or box shapes and work on the timing of the effect first. Once I'm happy with that, I'll look at scale and movement. After that comes the texture work. If it's a smoke plume, I'll look at creating an animated smoke texture that can be applied to the particles in the effect. Once all the elements have been brought together, I'll put the effect into the game.

Do you have any tips for surviving crunch?

Can's of fizzy drink.... Lots of cans of fizzy drink! And food... you've got to eat. On a serious side, if you're married or have a partner, having their support and understanding is vital. Crunch can sometimes mean that you don't get to see your wife and kids at all during the week. This can put a huge strain of life outside of work, so their support is essential. Also, having an understanding employer is important. If you're struggling with overtime and need a break, speak to you line-manager about it and see what can be done. Don't just sit there and burn yourself out. A team who are drained, tired and irritable will create more problems than solve them, so employers need to ensure that any crunch is managed effectively and not treated like a death march. Crunch is a part of development that is almost always inevitable. Due to the creative aspect of making a game, many developers want to create the best possible game they can and this often requires them to work extra hours to achieve that.

There's some good advice there. Since you mention the extra hours, what are the longest hours you've worked during a crunch?

24 hours. I brought my sleeping bag into the studio and slept on the floor once, but that was many, many years ago when I was single, so crunch really didn't bother me back then…..
I often stayed late even when I didn't need to. However, more recently, I've been fortunate enough not to have to work horrendous hours, so an average day during crunch, for me, is about 12hours (9 a.m. till 9 p.m.) and only when needed to do so.

If you could change one thing about the industry what would that be?

That's a good question….. I honestly don't know. Tax breaks in the U.K. would be nice. That would bring us back into a competitive market with Canada and the US.

How do you feel about the challenges women face in the industry?

Do women face a challenge in the industry? I've worked with many women over the years and they are always on an equal footing with men. Sure the industry has far more men working in it, but I don't see that as an issue for women at all. In fact, my current boss is a woman and she is very well respected and successful.

Do you think attitudes to women are changing in the industry?

Very much so as stated previously, there are more and more women getting involved in the industry. Seeing a woman walking about a studio is no longer a rare sight. I also believe that women in the industry are a very positive thing. Over recent years, we have seen far more family based and female orientated games come to market. I believe this is largely due to women's involvement in the industry. It is great news for the Industry as it's another sector of the market that can be tapped into, therefore strengthening the Industry as a whole.

Do you feel women need to work harder to prove themselves in the industry?

Not at all, I think many people's perceptions have changed over the years. For me, a good artist is a good artist... regardless of gender.

If you could offer one piece of advice to someone starting out in the industry what would that be?

Don't expect to be buying that Ferrari anytime soon. I mean that as a serious statement. The industry has grown massively over the past 25 years or so. It's now a proper, full blown industry. Long gone are the days of a budding game designer making a game in his (or her) bedroom and making millions. What I'm trying to say is, keep a clear head. If you really want to get into the industry, look into what part of the industry appeals to you. The games industry isn't just about the development. There's also Marketing, P.R., Administration etc. Look at the games that interest you and what companies make those games. Above all, have fun. The games industry can be very brutal at times and at others, very rewarding. It's not a hobby.... It's a career.

As part of this book I've been trying to highlight as many different possible career paths as I can and it does surprise me that there are just so many people involved with creating and supporting a game. Do you have any advice for people who can't decide what to do in the industry?

If you really want to be involved with the games industry, but are still unsure as to what you'd like to do, try contacting your local games development studio and see if they offer any work experience or internship positions. This will allow you to move around the studio and work with many different departments. Also research the games industry and what each job entails. There are many 'making of' documentaries about the games industry and these could offer more insight into the games industry. During my career, I've moved around in all different roles within the art studio, from Animation, Environment, Concept and VFX. This has allowed me to discover what areas I'm really interested in and where I'd like to see my career going forward. Don't be afraid to try different things and speak to your managers about possibly trying out alternative jobs within the studio. This may not always be possible due to project commitments, but don't be afraid to ask. When a new project starts, there may well be an opportunity for you to try something else. A lot of people fresh from school or college get into the games industry through game testing (Q.A.). This can be a great way for you to understand the development process of the games industry. However, Q.A. is a very important aspect of games development and shouldn't just be seen as a springboard or fast track into the industry.

Thanks for your time Pete it's been great catching up on what you've been up to.

Name:	Nathan McCree	*Currently working for:*	Vatra Games
Age:	43	*Current role:*	Audio Director
Sex:	Male	*Length of Service:*	1.5 years

Nathan and I worked together in Brighton. Nathan is a talented and experienced Audio Engineer. We caught up to find out what advice he could offer to the budding musicians out there.

Why did you want to get into the games industry?

It wasn't really something I had planned. I had always liked games from an early age, programming my own stuff on a Sinclair ZX81 and then later on a BBC Micro. I also had a very healthy appetite for writing my own music and creating sounds. I saw the games industry as a way to mix both my programming skills and my addiction to all things audio.

What do you do in the industry?

I am a composer and sound designer. Currently I am the Audio Director for Vatra Games in Brno, Czech Republic.

How long have you worked in the industry?

19 years.

Who have you worked for in the industry?

Core Design, 8th Day, Codo Technologies, Lost Toys, Brat Designs, Lionhead Studios, Custom Play Games, Three, Headstrong, Circle Studios, Zoe Mode, Gusto Games, Crush Digital, Vatra, Konami

That's quite a list of companies. Do you have any preference between publishers or developers and why?

Not really – work is work at the end of the day. It's safer working directly with a publisher – they are less likely to go bust, but if I had to make a preference it would probably be working with developers. I like being on the shop floor and getting my hands dirty.

I remember Core Design, sadly no longer with us. I guess most people are interested in how the music actually arrives in the game so could your briefly explain the process for us?

Well it usually starts with some idea for style. Sometimes it's very specific like "We want John Williams, Star Wars music", or "We want Edward Scissorhands". Other times it can be vague and ambiguous. I remember one time I was asked to write the music for a stone-aged/dinosaur cross breed. The music brief was literally this "We want tribal music but we don't want it tribal." Crazy! Anyway, once you have someone's idea for style (and sometimes no one has any idea at all and you have to find a style for the game yourself) then usually some temp track is put into the game to test the style. A temp track is a term we use for a piece of music that is classed as a placeholder. If the tests are successful and the Creative Director is happy then you can start to think about a composer. It may be you or it may be someone else who is more suited to producing that kind of style. A music brief is then put together and interviews take place. There are many different ways of implementing music into a game. So it's not always the same job. Sometimes it is a collection of about 15 three minute pieces. Other times it can be over a hundred tiny fragments which are joined together by the audio engine making the music interact more closely with exactly what is happening at any given moment. Another way to implement music into a game is to play several tracks simultaneously, cross-fading between each track and combining tracks in order to create different textures in real-time. The implementation method is very much dependant on the genre of the game, memory constraints, available code support and of course the composer's ability to produce the cues according to the music brief. Once the cues have been delivered they are usually connected to cues which are used by code and/or the audio engine to trigger pieces of music, either looping or one-shot, cross-fading, interrupting etc. The list of rules which governs how the music is executed can be lengthy. This particular audio system should be well thought out, designed and documented if it is to achieve a good result.

Do you still get to create music as an Audio Director or is your time occupied by other managerial tasks?

Funny you should ask that as I have been considering assigning the music to me for our next game at Vatra. It is just a thought at the moment. I need to sit down with the project plan and audio schedule to decide whether it is something I would have time to do. To answer your question, since I have been Audio Director I have hardly created a thing. Most of my time is spent organising my staff and contractors. I do a lot of talking with the team. I'm basically a problem solver now. It is also my job to keep the audio on the right creative track, so I'm still being creative but more in an advisory role.

What would you say is the highlight of your career so far?

The pinnacle of my game releases would have to be Tomb Raider I, II and III. The highlight of my career so far would be going to Hollywood Bowl to see the L.A. Philharmonic Orchestra perform 2 tracks from the Tomb Raider soundtrack (amongst other games music) in front of 11,000 people.

So what would you consider the lowlight of your career so far?

Setting up my own Music and Sound Production Company – I didn't get paid for 2 years!

How did you originally get into the industry and did you do anything unique to increase your chances?

I was looking for a programming job straight out of college. I imagined I would end up in some business software development company. I sent out about 200 job applications, I got a few interviews here and there, mostly insurance and communications companies and then there was this one game development company in Derby, Core Design Ltd. I succeeded in the interview and started my first job in the games industry as a Junior Programmer. After six months of programming a music sequencer for the Sega Mega-Drive, I wrote some music on it to demonstrate the software. My boss liked it so much he asked me to write the rest of the music for the game, Asterix and the Great Rescue. I have been writing music and creating sound effects for games ever since.

How did you get into your current role?

In the summer of 2010 I was working as the Audio Manager for Zoe Mode in Brighton. My Director at the time asked me if I would be prepared to provide some extra audio support for one of our sister companies in Brno, Czech Republic, Vatra Games. Initially it was for a 3 month contract, but while I was there I saw that there was a significant lack of in-house audio resources. I had a conversation with the studio head at the time, Matthew Seymour and suggested that he hire me full-time. He agreed so we began negotiating the practicalities of my relocation and my eventual full-time position as Audio Director, which started in November 2010.

What advice would you give to people looking to be an Audio Director in the industry?

Get a good show reel sorted out. Show as many different aspects of your creativity as possible without boring people to death. Show excerpts rather than full-length pieces. Most people's concentration is lost after only 30 seconds if their interest is not kept up. Show Sound Design examples as well as Music. Most people wanting to work in computer games audio also secretly want to be the next superstar composer. We do not need wannabe superstar composers. We need audio designers with strong programming, logic and communication skills with a flair for composition. For people who are using the games industry as a 'way in' to becoming a famous rock star or Hollywood composer, they should look elsewhere.

So is it possible to work in the audio field without programming skills?

Yes it is possible. Lots of the guys that work for me have no programming skills at all. It limits what I can use them for but that's not usually a problem. Having said that, the more skill sets you have the more indispensible you are and in this economic climate that's not a bad thing.

If hiring would you put more emphasis on education or experience?

That depends on the position that I am looking to fill. If I am looking for a junior, then someone with good qualifications is the starting point, but I would be looking for a special creative flair too. If I am looking for someone senior then it is more about experience and their track record. Personal recommendations play an important part too. Somebody can be tooled up with all the education, experience and creative flair you could ask for, but if they have an attitude problem or are difficult to work with in some way then usually it's better to find someone else. Making games is all about being part of a team so new members of that team need to fit in and play their part efficiently and cooperatively.

Do you have any final thoughts for people hoping to become an Audio Director in the games industry?

Prepare yourself for some long nights, weekend work, unpaid overtime and lots of pizza. If you can handle that you will have a great time.

With regards to actually working in the industry, what would you say is the best thing about your role?

I guess the best thing is mentoring other sound designers and then (hopefully) hearing them improve and create great assets and audio systems. Also working with the latest technologies and software is a big buzz. I guess I'm a bit of a geek at heart!

What's the worst thing about your role?

Working lengthy crunch periods can be very draining and demoralizing, not to mention a heavy burden on one's social life. Improper memory constraints / management can also make the job frustrating, having to sacrifice quality and detail because of hardware limitations or insufficient project planning is never pleasant.

I always get annoyed by quality taking a dive due to memory constraints. Do you think that's becoming a thing of the past with our hardware improvements or will it always be around?

It should be a thing of the past already. Memory is so small and cheap now that I believe the next gen. consoles will take a giant leap forward. However I'm not sure that increasing the memory will make the problem go away. If you give developers more memory, they tend to use it.

So what's an average day for an Audio Director like?

8:45 a.m. – arrive at work, make a coffee. Check previous day's work by audio design team. Provide feedback via emails to the rest of the team before they arrive at 10 a.m. Ensure daily tasks for the team are properly assigned and update the audio schedule as necessary.
10:30 a.m. – attend daily leads meeting.
11:00 a.m. – attend project leads meeting.

11:30 a.m. – provide support for audio team members, removing blockages where possible and reassigning tasks where appropriate.

12:00 noon – answer emails.

1:00 p.m. – lunch.

2:00 p.m. – work on my own project specific tasks while responding to any audio requests that come into the department throughout the day. This can include assigning immediate tasks to other team members, audio for trailer movies, fixing bugs, recording live sound assets, answering emails, attending emergency meetings, discussing new ideas with programmers, artists, designers and animators etc.

5:00 p.m. – update project management software.

5:30p. m. – a brief chat with team members to review how the day has gone.

6:00 p.m. – finish.

Do you have any tips for surviving crunch?

Get some sleep. Don't be tempted by going to the pub every night in order to 'wind down'. Sometimes it can be difficult to get to sleep when your adrenaline is high. Try doing some exercise instead or reading a good book after a hot bath. You will go to sleep eventually and it's better to get 6 good hours than 8 or 9 hours tanked up with alcohol. Try to alternate late/early nights at the office. Remember to eat well. Too much junk food can sap your energy, making the whole experience even harder. When the crunch is over, take a holiday.

So what are the longest hours you've worked during a crunch?

Probably my longest straight would be something like 36 hours, but that is quite rare. Usually a crunch period would necessitate 10 to 16 hours per day. It is actually almost impossible to maintain 12, let alone 16 hours every day, but it can be achieved in short bursts. So maybe 3 days of 12 to 14 hours, followed by 2 days at 10 hours per day can be expected sometimes with one extra day at the weekend and one day off. This kind of crunching can be quite common for the closing 2 or 3 months of a project though sometimes this can be extended to 6 or more months if the project is not managed properly.

If you could change one thing about the industry what would that be?

If I could change one thing it would have to be the assumption and expectation that development staff should work overtime and crunch without any reward or remuneration simply because they love doing what they do.

Do you think that with advancements like the day-one patch that we might soon see an end to the crunch periods of games development?

I think that crunch periods can be minimized by good project management, but I'm not sure that you can eradicate it altogether. Ultimately making a game is a creative process and with most creative processes there is never an end. Things can always be polished and perfected a little more. If a team cares about its project and the developing company treats its staff fairly, I think there is a natural desire to put in some extra hours to make it as good as possible. The day-one patch may be a good remedy for crunching, but I don't think it is the cure.

How do you feel about the challenges women face in the industry?

I think the challenges are fair and I believe there are many opportunities within the games industry which can be filled easily by women. It is not physical work so there is no advantage being male. It is about having the experience, track record, logic and creative flair to pursue new ideas. About having a vision for something, being able to communicate that vision to other team members and having a willingness to discuss other possibilities and solutions.

Do you think attitudes to women are changing in the industry?

Yes I think so. Personally I have worked with some very talented and creative women and I would not hesitate to work with those people again.

Do you feel women need to work harder to prove themselves in the industry?

No I don't think so. As long as they are as productive and as professional as their male counterparts then that is all I would expect.

If you could offer one piece of advice to someone starting out in the industry what would that be?

Don't just know about your discipline (Audio, Art, Animation, Code, Design, Q.A., Production); get to know what the others do and how the whole team fits together. The more you know about the other disciplines the easier it will be to find solutions for what is in effect, the newest and most exciting industry of our age!

Name:	Andrew Smith	*Currently working for:*	Spilt Milk Studios
Age:	29	*Current role:*	Founder/Designer
Sex:	Male	*Length of Service:*	1.5 years

When I worked in Scotland we took on a keen young tester and over the years I've watched Andrew develop his skills from Q.A. into design and finally starting out with his own studio.

Why did you want to get into the games industry?

Ever since I was a kid videogames fascinated me. I'm a frustrated storyteller even now, a big part of storytelling is world building. Games opened up a window into countless wonderful, mesmerizing worlds ripe for exploration. Ever since I saw Pacman in a Swiss hotel when I was about 6 years old they've held a magical power over me. I never wanted to do anything else.

How long have you worked in the industry?

About seven and a half years, give or take. Started in Q.A. as so many designers do and worked my way up!

Who have you worked for in the industry?

HASBRO Interactive, Acclaim Studios (in Cheltenham), Vis, Visual Science, Realtime Worlds, Proper Games and my own company, Spilt Milk Studios.

What do you do in the industry?

I'm a Game Designer by training and by trade. I make levels, write documents, tweak variables, manage the broad elements of games in development. More recently I've been forced into managing outsourcing of code, art, sound and Q.A., as well as P.R. and Marketing. It's been a trial by fire, but I've been really enjoying pushing myself.

Do you feel that the start you had in Q.A. has helped you in your role as a designer?

Absolutely! In Q.A. you get to see so many varied facets of a game's creation, from the very beginning to the very end. This gives you an insight that helps a designer, at the very least, relate to all of the different skill sets and kinds of people who have input into a game over its lifetime. It also lets you see all the wonderful ways things can go wrong and all of the tiny ways in which small changes can have huge effects to a project, not only in terms of game-play and user experience, but also in terms of budget and project management.

What would you say is the highlight of your career so far?

There have been a few memorable moments. Pitching Flock! to Adam Boyes at Capcom was nerve wracking and exciting, especially because it led to a publishing deal. Winning a Scottish BAFTA for the same game was also immensely exciting. However, releasing my own game (a joint collaboration with Nicoll Hunt) on iPhone was the highlight... seeing it from start to finish, under my own company's banner, seeing the positive reception was just an amazing experience. I've always been personally invested in the games I make, but not only was this game special it was my company's first original creation.

So what would you consider the lowlight of your career so far?

The lowlight was likely an episode where a company I'd worked for made a turn for the worse. It had employed someone who did not really understand or appreciate the company's culture in a senior position and this led to a slow and painful downfall. The company's still going, which is great, it has moved on, but it was heartbreaking to see how such a tight-knit team was torn apart by one bad decision. Nobody could've seen it coming, but nothing was done to minimize the impact, such a shame.

How did you originally get into the industry and did you do anything unique to increase your chances?

I was lucky enough to get some Q.A. summer jobs while at university, but the key difference between me and any other people with that experience was my modding. As a hobby I made levels and modifications for Half Life and Unreal Tournament. Actually finishing these things is a huge bonus on your C.V. Not only that, we entered a team into the Dare to be Digital competition hosted at Abertay, Dundee. All of these elements added up and I found myself a Junior Level Design role!

Earlier on we mention modding as a good thing for future designers to be doing. Did this give you enough knowledge to start in a design role or was it case of having to learn all over again?

The skills you learn creating levels for, as I did, an FPs isn't exclusive to first person games. Sure, some of the skills and tricks are only really relevant to that kind of game, but more broad rules like polygon counts, readability, the method of designing on paper, then white-boxing, then moving forward into full production are all applied every day to any game you work on. It's invaluable.

How did you get into your current role?

I left the company I was working for, set up my own! Simple as that really! I'll admit it was a bit hasty but I just felt that if I didn't make the jump when I did, I never would and would always regret. So yeah, the simplest way to become a managing director is to set up your own company... but it's hard to run a company (even a company of one!) so the people who can't handle it become very easy to spot.

What was scarier the first interview for a job in the industry or your first day on the job at Split Milk?

The first day on the job as Spilt Milk Studios was so busy and happened so seamlessly that I barely noticed a change. I felt good, but it was a few weeks before the stress kicked in! The first interview I went to was by far the scariest thing ever. Since then I've found them easier and I've also moved over to the other side of the table now during any interviews that happen.

What advice would you give to people looking to start their own company in the industry?

Work hard, get enough experience, don't wed yourself to a regular paycheque. I've not paid myself properly since starting up and have made a lot of lifestyle sacrifices to be where I am right now and there's still a lot of work to do before I become 'successful'. It takes the minimum of two years to build a successful or stable company, so if you're not ready (psychologically, mentally, financially or creatively) to make that kind of commitment then be very careful. That said; don't leave it so long that you balk at the idea of spending 2 years without steady income. It's hard to say with certainty when is right, but for me I just knew it when the time came.

If hiring would you put more emphasis on education or experience?

Experience outweighs education, every time. That's why hobby projects are so crucial. If you're applying for a games' job in this day and age, without some working, playable proof of a game you've worked on, then you're likely not to land the job. There are so many easy ways to get hands on experience creating a videogame (and selling them via iTunes or on websites) that there really is no excuse. If you haven't got this sort of experience already and you're making excuses, then you're doing yourself a huge disservice.

So would you consider a decent, polished show reel essential in the job market?

A show reel is all you have when it comes down to it. This is the thing that shows your practical skills off and a polished reel (or level, or game) goes to elevate you above everyone else vying for your job. You have to remember you're not only trying to prove yourself capable and employable, you're competing with a ton of other people who you have to assume have very similar skill-sets. So then it comes down to how you present those skills that counts.

Do you have any final thoughts for people hoping to start their own games business?

Have faith in your ability. Without experience you'll have confidence though and confidence is that thing that helps you get through all the aspects of running a business that you haven't yet experienced. Also, don't be afraid to make mistakes, it's the fastest way to learn after all!

With regards to actually working in the industry, what would you say is the best thing about being a designer?

As a designer it's being able to come up with an interesting idea, visualize it, communicate it and then see it work. The end result is obviously seeing other people smile as they play your game and that's still the greatest buzz of all. That's what keeps me going late at night.

What's the worst thing about your role?

Not being able to code! Honestly that's more of a problem with my personal skill set. Being a designer is great except when people who don't understand your value on a project come to question it. Which happens more than you'd think, I can't count the amount of times I've had to justify decisions and fight my corner when things get tough? Coders and artists don't really understand that element because their work is way more obvious and more easily quantifiable. That said it's all great practice, half of a game designer's job is to communicate effectively after all!

So what's an average day for you like?

As a designer it starts with emails and then before lunch I'll get stuck into documentation. It's also very rare that a day goes past without a design element being implemented in a game and the need arises for you to check, play test and re-balance the element in question. The biggest common thread of my average day though is being torn violently from one issue to another, repeatedly and with no warning. I constantly have to reprioritize my to-do list... but I'm not sure I'd like it any other way. The odd days where I just get to sit undisturbed with a document of level design to do is a relief though.

Do you have any tips for surviving crunch?

Don't do it! Seriously, the only reason I crunch is because I'm the only employee, it's my company. Any company that asks you to crunch is to be treated with distrust and sometimes contempt. It's just a form of workplace exploitation. That said, if you do get forced into it, make sure you have a full day away from screens of any kind at least once a week.

So what are the longest hours you've worked during a crunch?

Once I worked a full 48hr. shift, ended up hallucinating. Also managed to race an entire Championship Cup (6 races?!) asleep. Or at least in a state which means I only remembering starting and then finishing. That was in Q.A. I've done lots of crunch since, but it's not something that is healthy, either for you as a person, the project itself, or the company. Crunch is evil.

But is crunch a necessary evil in the industry?

I don't believe it is necessary at all. The industry has spent too long relying on it. I don't think it's entirely possible to remove occasional longer hours from a company with complete certainty, but crunch is different. Crunch is extended, negative and

thing is the more companies adopt a stance against the culture of
more companies who do let it slip into their culture will start seeing
lling to work for them. It's only a matter of time before it goes away.

nge one thing about the industry what would that be?

The attitude to crunch is one thing. But also I'd like to see a more varied group of people developing. It'll come in time, but more girls and ethnicities would only be a good thing. Their influences would spread and our audience would expand too.

How do you feel about the challenges women face in the industry?

I think it's a shame they face any at all, but they do. I personally know of several women in the industry who've been victim of discrimination of one form or another and loads more who feel like they need to prove something or otherwise perform differently to their male counterparts. I even lean slightly towards positive discrimination when talking about recruiting. More women in the games industry can only be a good thing.

Do you think attitudes to women are changing in the industry?

Slowly but surely, yes. It should change more quickly though!

Do you feel women need to work harder to prove themselves in the industry?

I don't think they need to work harder to prove themselves, but I think a lot of women feel that way and a lot of men in the industry have a really skewed view and attitude that only encourages it.

If you could offer one piece of advice to someone starting out in the industry what would that be?

Hard work pays off, but don't find yourself in a place where you're being exploited.

Finally where do you see Spilt Milk further down the road?

Ultimately I see a core of a few very talented and multi-disciplined people with outsourcing playing a large role. I want to be a multi-game studio with a few respected and healthy-selling franchises under our belt. I never want to stop trying original work, but the reality of business means I'd hope to have a fallback on a popular series. That we own the IP of, naturally!

Andrew it's been a pleasure to see you go from testing to owning your own company. I'll be watching out for what you bring out next and on behalf of the readers and myself, thanks for your time.

Name:	Rhys Twelves	**Currently working for:**	Bioware
Age:	38	**Current role:**	Lead Programmer
Sex:	Male	**Length of Service:**	6 months

Rhys is a very good friend of mine and an extremely talented coder. We met when we were both temping at Climax, since then he has worked for some of the best studios in the industry.

Why did you want to get into the games industry?

It's all I ever wanted to do, make games. Before that when I was a kid I wanted to be either an Architect or join the R.A.F. Once I got into computer programming (at about 13/14) I was hooked.

How long have you worked in the industry?

16 years

Who have you worked for in the industry?

Codemasters, TT-Games, Kuju, Splash Damage, Infogrames/Gremlin, Visual Science. Contracted for a few others inc. Monumental/ Blue-52/ Genemation & Big Red Games

Wow, that's quite a range of companies. Do you prefer a publisher or developer and why?

There are pros and cons to both. Working for a publisher you have fewer stakeholders to please and issues can be resolved quickly. The down-side can be that projects can spend a long time in development, but then get canned as they either:

a) Pick up a hot title and push everything into that. An example of this would be Infogrames when they got the Matrix trilogy game license or

b) A game no longer fits with a publishers 'image'. An example of this would be Black Rock Studios when they became owned by Disney.

As a developer you don't get those issues too much as you get generally more creative freedom, can shop around for publishers if the fit is not right and you don't usually can long-in-development projects unless something is VERY wrong with it. Also, you tend to be more careful about projects you do start up in the first place. A down-side to being just a development studio is the work-for-hire scenario where small studios are forced to take anything that is going to keep afloat. When that happens, the studio will struggle to find and retain good staff as they don't want to work on "Babies High School Adventures" or "Let's cook Thai with Emma B".

Having worked on a Miley Cyrus game I can relate to that, not that I'm saying anything is wrong with Miley Cyrus games. Moving along what do you do in the industry?

I'm a Lead Programmer so I write code for various systems. I architect systems, mentor juniors, work with other Leads.

What would you say is the highlight of your career so far?

I am there working for one of the most respected development studios in the industry (Bioware). If I wasn't at the high-point I'd be thinking of getting out of the industry. It's a short-lived career, so when you feel you have reached a peak or are on the other side of that peak, then it's probably time to get out.

So why do you think you'd be leaving the industry after having worked in it for over a decade?

I always thought it was a young man's game. Even when I first got in it, I thought "Well, we'll see how I get on, but I would expect a younger, hungrier breed to be overtaking me with 4th or 5th generation coding skills within the next 5 years". It didn't quite happen that way. Methods, processes and languages didn't accelerate at the same speed as the hardware, but I've always kept with that opinion that when I'm too old to cut the mustard it's better to step off the train. I just don't want to be the guy in the corner looking like a well-worn pack-horse sent out to pasture.

Interesting, so what would you consider the lowlight of your career so far?

Hmm . . . . Tricky… 2 I think:

 1) Renting a room in my boss's house. That was HELL, tip: Never do it. If you can never get away from work, as it follows you home, you'll go insane.

2) Spending months away from my family writing a PS2 engine from scratch without any assistance from a Lead or other experienced programmers and then being made to feel like a scapegoat for why the milestones were not achieved on time.

How did you originally get into the industry?

After coming back to England having spent 2.5 years in general I.T. Consultancy and working in Holland for 6 months, I reflected on what I wanted. I remembered why I got into programming in the first place and decided I would get into the games industry at all costs. So I went for an interview at Codemasters in Leamington Spa, U.K., got a job as a graphics programmer there.

Did you do anything unique to stand out from other applicants?

I did actually. Looking back on it, it was probably a cheap shot and with the upsurge in agencies and electronic media, probably not possible now. I had a friend who owned a professional printing firm making brochures. I had done some work for him over the summer making some custom business accounting and management software applications and for payment I asked if he would make me a brochure quality, custom designed C.V. It was a master-stroke. From that one small effort, I ended up having more interviews than I could actually attend and one of the most common questions the interviewers asked "Where did you get your C.V. printed?"

I was asked to give advice to people wanting to get in the industry now? If you have time write a demo, alone, take it to interview on a USB stick, laptop, whatever. Make sure it is just your work, be prepared to show & explain source code, answer questions on design, etc. If an employer can see your work first hand, rather than read summaries about it on a C.V. then they will be able to ascertain a lot more about what type of employee you will be and how useful you will be to a team. E.g. As a programmer, your C.V may show training in Physics or Networking, but a demo may show that you have a knack for graphics or UI. Showing off working code will always stand you out from the crowd of people who know programming, but don't have a passion for game programming.

How did you get into your current role?

After a recommendation from a friend who worked here, I applied for a role that was open, passed the tests and seemed to do O.K. with the interviews (telephone & face-to-face).

What advice would you give to people looking to be a lead programmer in the industry?

Ask around first. Many people have preconceptions of what is involved in the games industry, it's mostly wrong. Not many people spend all day playing games, those that do (Q.A.) have a very special talent, not for playing 'games', but for playing the same game (mostly in a broken/development state) for an extended period of time and finding errors & problems with it. The rewarding aspect of it (seeing your work on shelves in shops, top of the game charts or being reported about in the national news) is very short-lived and the period between those moments very long (2+ years). Since you will be working with extremely talented individuals in all disciplines don't expect much praise for your work. Excellence is expected, only a rare few stand out from the crowd.

If hiring, would you put more emphasis on education or experience?

A bit of both. A strong educational background is very useful for some disciplines (Math., Art, Design, etc.), but then there are people who have just gone feet-first into their careers without requiring certificates of confirmation and can be equally useful to teams in this industry. When interviewing I look for cognitive processes in a candidate. How do they start working on a problem? What are the steps they take? Are they logical or gut reaction, do they struggle without guidance? Can they explain well how they are thinking? The C.V. is one thing and can scream genius, but a quick explorative conversation can reveal more about a person than all the jobs & education he has had will.

Any final thoughts for people hoping to become a lead programmer in the games industry?

Be sure you want it. It can be a lonely place if you feel you don't really fit in. It's hard work that's for sure and outside of the media industry and some niche technology areas, the games industry is not really regarded as a serious profession. If you've spent

1 year hating your job in the industry, I wouldn't be thinking "I'll stick with it for another year as it will look good on my C.V." as other industries (other than those mentioned) won't see the experience as very valid. Harsh, but in my experience, people coming out of the games industry find it difficult to get positions at their similar level.

In that case would you say a career in the games industry is one for life?

If you're lucky enough, then yes. The industry has gotten so much bigger now than the early days of games being written by 2 coders in a bedroom, with your mum bringing up meals (to make sure you ate) and hand-packaging CDs/Tapes in boxes, but if you really enjoy all the good parts about being in it, then it can be very rewarding and there is rarely a dull moment.

With regards to working in the industry in modern times, what would you say is the best thing about your role?

It's an infant industry, so it's always changing. You always have to keep abreast of new things and so it rarely gets stale to any great degree. You get to play with brand new prototype hardware. Playing with new stuff, blowing it up...
You cannot ask for more than that.

What's the worst thing about your role?

Being needed 48 hours in a day.
Supporting other developers, discussing issues with other team's, leads, etc. It just means you can never fit time in your normal day to get your own work done. I actually like programming, so the less and less I do, the unhappier I get.

So, do you regret climbing the career ladder then?

It's par for the course. I knew it would be tough. Friends who made the jump before me would always mention how difficult it was to get any programming done anymore and some became almost entirely 'hands-off' as they knew any time spent 'in' the code was wasted as they would get pulled out into more strategic meetings before being able to finish off entire subsystems. I promised myself I would remain 'hands-on' and so far have managed that. Personally, I think that the industry needs to address roles within it as games teams become ever larger and decide where the best 'bang-

Do you feel women need to work harder to prove themselves in the industry?

Not in games. It is a very results focused industry. It's less about personality and more about how good you are at your job. I can't speak for all disciplines as I'm more exposed to programming than other areas, but in my experience when people judge other people it's down to their code (or other work) and not their dress sense, demeanour, or personality.

If you could offer one piece of advice to someone starting out in the industry what would that be?

Be prepared to continue studying. It doesn't stop after your schooling. This industry changes so quickly, you have to keep learning all the time.

Thanks for your time

No problem. Glad to be of help.

Name:	Barry Northern	*Currently working for:*	4T2 Entertainment
Age:	34	*Current role:*	Senior Game Developer
Sex:	Male	*Length of Service:*	3 months

Barry is another ex-colleague of mine, one of the nicest programmers in the industry.

Why did you want to get into the games industry?

I never considered anything else. I worked on games since before I was 10, starting out from typing in BASIC code from books into my ZX Spectrum 16K. Making games seemed to be the only thing worth doing with computers.

How long have you worked in the industry?

Professionally for over 13 years.

Who have you worked for in the industry?

Rare, Relentless (Freelance), Climax, Kuju and 4T2

What do you do in the industry?

Code, technical design, I organize work-flows and procedures, provide technical assistance, manage code teams.

What would you say is the highlight of your career so far?

Personally I think coding Chime Super Deluxe.

So what would you consider the lowlight of your career so far?

My failed attempt at starting up my own games company with a couple of friends could be considered one. But I'd do it again as I learned a lot. I don't see it as a lowlight really.

I imagine you would learn a hell of a lot attempting your own business. What piece of advice would you give others considering this route?

If you work with others, make sure they are 100% committed and willing to put in the effort. Also make sure you are. Also make sure that you are all singing from the same song sheet. Keep it simple. If you can, only start once you already have work lined up. Don't expand too quickly. Keep your overheads as low as possible, but do everything by the book. If you haven't got a head for business, make sure you have someone you trust who does. Make sure you're doing it for reasons that feel right to you, are for the good of you and of everyone else involved.

How did you originally get into the industry?

I did a degree in Computer Visualization and Animation at Bournemouth University's National Centre for Computer Animation, wrote a small C++ games engine on UNIX graphics boxes, which were the same ones they used at Rare. That, coupled with my experience of making game since I was small, secured my first paid role.

How did you get into your current role?

I decided I wanted to work there, went to the interview, got the job. This was because I have 13 years console experience, lead experience on multiple projects and moreover because I showed that I still absolutely love creating the best, most perfect games I can and working in the industry.

What advice would you give to people looking to be a senior game developer in the industry?

Turn your attention instead to always strive to create something new that people will think is cool.

So you would say you shouldn't set your sights to making games, but set them to being creative and original in whatever aspect of games creation you're involved in?

Not at all. You should definitely set your sights on making the best games you can. Never lose sight of the big picture. The best trick you can learn is to focus on the detail, on your specific task in the moment, whilst simultaneously knowing what is going on over the whole project, what has gone on, what will go on (or at least, what is planned). Never say: "It's not my responsibility". The whole game is your responsibility.

If hiring would you put more emphasis on education or experience?

Experience whatever the level. It is possible for people to get on and make things. They need to have done that, to have loved doing it, to have learned a lot from it that they won't forget.

So would you say an education is pointless or does that depend on the discipline?

Of course education is not pointless. It is a necessary foundation. It is crucial for any discipline that you learn as much as possible both generally and specifically and keep learning. Education doesn't stop when work starts.

So it's ongoing process for us all, which make sense when you consider the ever changing technology behind the games we play. Do you have any final thoughts for people hoping to become a senior games developer in the games industry?

Do your job well, help everyone else do their jobs well too.

Good advice, it's all about being a part of and supporting the team, with regards to actually working in the industry. What would you say is the best thing about your role?

I get paid for doing something I'd be doing anyway.

What's the worst thing about your role?

Occasional periods of intense crunch, which are getting harder to recover from the older I get.

So what's an average day for a games developer like?

For a professional games developer the average day consists of trying to get the scheduled work done, it taking too long, getting pulled in other directions by more pressing things that you never can plan for and then having a really good day when everything seems to come together and it all works itself out. There's a lot of working for varying periods of intense concentration on one's own and having to switch modes to help people and get things sorted in the team. I've got good at switching modes quickly. It doesn't do to be a diva, to be fussy about noise, to be unable to concentrate or resent having to stop what you're doing and go back to it later.

Do you have any tips for surviving crunch?

Think ahead, try to get the hard stuff done early. Don't cut corners, but do the job properly (you'll pay for it later otherwise), don't get stressed, it doesn't help. Also, don't be afraid to stand up and say enough is enough when you need to. As long as you've done a good job and worked hard up to that point, you deserve and require a break. Crunch should never last longer than two or three weeks. If it lasts more than a month there's something seriously wrong with the project and probably with the company. If it happens consistently, find another job unless it's in your power to make changes within the company.

So what are the longest hours you've worked during a crunch?

I don't really keep score, but for a recent vertical slice I was doing nearly 50 hour weeks for about three weeks. I can't do it for long, my work begins to suffer any more than that.

So is the video game industry for younger folk?

No. What I call "crunch" is a management mistake. Don't work for a company that is in continual or frequent crunch unless you can manage your work-life balance in a way that suits you and everyone else involved (work, family, friends) or you believe you have the ability to effect change at your company to help improve the lives of everyone that way. As creators, we should all be dedicated to making great things and every creative process requires periods of intense activity to bring the work up to a certain standard. You need to learn to recognize when extra work is needed for the good of the thing you're making and when time is being wasted through inefficient practices.

How do you feel about the challenges women face in the industry?

What challenges? The women I've met in the industry all seemed to get on just as well as the blokes.

Do you think attitudes to women are changing in the industry?

I think the average age of the team members has increased over the years. We're a more mature and sensible bunch now. Our attitude reflects my personal change in attitude from sniggering teenager to married man and there are a few more women now than there were. I don't believe there are any barriers to entry for women into the industry other than perhaps individual women who may not like working in a primarily male environment or who just might not like games. However, the types of game being made have become much more diverse and less male-oriented in the last five or six years.

Do you feel women need to work harder to prove themselves in the industry?

No. The quality of the work is all that matters.

If you could offer one piece of advice to someone starting out in the industry what would that be?

Think about what people would like to play with and get on with it. Don't make excuses, make games, don't be presumptuous, it's harder than it looks to get it right as the devil is in the detail.

Name:	Sherri Graner Ray	**Currently working for:**	Schell Games
Age:	NA	**Current role:**	Studio Design Director
Sex:	Female	**Length of Service:**	3 months

I met Sherri through Women in Games, an incredibly experienced designer who is well respected in the industry.

Why did you want to get into the games industry?

I didn't... exactly. When I got in to the industry there really wasn't an "industry" to get in to. It was a new idea, in Austin, Texas this was limited to one company, Origin Systems. But when I had the opportunity, I was such a great lover of table top games, that I saw computer games as an extension of that. I've got to admit, I never EVER would have believed I would still be doing it 21 years later!

Who have you worked for in the industry?

Warren Specter hired me in at Origin Systems. Since then I've worked with Electronic Arts, American Laser Games, Her Interactive, Sony Online Entertainment, Cartoon Network, Kings Isle, The US military/DoD, Kraft Foods and a host of others including my own company, twice.

Origin Systems was one of my favourite companies growing up. What was it like working in the industry back then compared to modern times and has it handled the transition to big business well enough?

Working for Origin back then was the golden days of game design. We could make the games we wanted with little to no interference from marketing, licenses or outside partners. I mean, seriously, if someone pitched Ultima today, who would buy in to it? "O.K...we're gonna do these games about this guy called The Avatar... and he works for this king called Lord British who lives in Britannia... ". They'd be laughed out of the office today! So we got to do really fun, creative things.

However, pay and quality of life were really not good. I was being paid $14,000 a year at Origin. Yes, it was 20 years ago, but even then that was barely a living wage and because we didn't have any control, the designs changed wildly on a daily basis. Crunch time was rampant and uncompensated.

So, today we may have a little less creative freedom, we have good wages, less crunch time and much better quality of life which is simply better overall.

Warren Specter is one of those known names in the industry. Why do you think certain people have made a name for themselves in what is otherwise a nameless industry?

Well the "nameless-ness" was a conscious decision on the industry's part. I was there when conversations were actually going on among the executives on whether or not it was good for the industry to have "rock stars", that is people who put their name on boxes to help sales "Richard Garriott's Ultima" "Chris Robert's Wing Commander", but ultimately it was decided by the execs. that having "rock stars" was not a good idea in the long run as it held the company hostage to the "rock star" persona.

However, there are some people who have still managed to become a "name" such as Warren or Richard or Sid or Will. The reason for their longevity, I believe, is because of the role their talent played in shaping the industry into what it is today.

What do you do in the industry?

I have served as everything from a production designer to head of product development. I have also served as C.E.O. of my own company. But my love is design and I have spent the majority of my time as a designer.

What would you say is the highlight of your career so far?

I was at GDC two years ago when a woman came up to me. She smiled and introduced herself and said, "I don't expect you to remember me, but I wanted to thank you personally. I was at GDC last year, trying to decide if this was the career I wanted. I met you and you were so warm and welcoming, you made me feel so comfortable and told me that you were sure I could make it here that I decided to give it a try. I'm now a programmer at (big name company here) and I owe it all to you."

That must have been really nice, I personally love to see people who started as a junior moving onwards and upwards. What would you consider the lowlight of your career so far?

When I was working at Sony Online Entertainment and they told us to implement the NGE for Star Wars Galaxies, 'nuff said.

I've seen some insane decisions by designers over the years. Do you feel that publishers often lead the game down a misguided path or is it just a case of their money, their choice?

I don't think anyone purposefully sets up a team or a project to fail. Usually there is a cascade of things that happen. The team over promises and under produces, the execs have spent money to advertise, advertisers are waiting, investors want their money or to see their project. Many things can happen. Finally, it has a lot to do with the age of this industry. We are all still learning and, unfortunately, that sometimes takes its toll on the projects themselves.

How did you originally get into the industry and did you do anything unique to increase your chances?

I was lucky enough to live in Austin, Texas, where Origin Systems was. I met a person at a little local gaming convention who worked there and he asked to join my weekly paper game group. I said yes and after several months of playing together (I ran the games) he told me he liked all the stuff I wrote and designed for our game and thought I would be a natural fit for the "writer" position at his company. He took in my resume and two weeks later I had an interview with Warren Specter. Two weeks after that I started at Origin as a writer on the Ultima series. That was in 1989.

What advice would you give to people looking to be a design director in the industry?

Network and volunteer.

By networking I mean go to every game industry event you can. Use Facebook and Twitter. Join the IGDA. Attend any and all game industry oriented events and stay in contact with those people you meet

By volunteering. There is NO better way to be involved than to volunteer to help with the IGDA events and/or conference events. The very best job? Handing out nametags! You get to put names to faces, second best job: setting up and manning a room for speakers, gives you a bit of invaluable face time with some very important industry people!

If hiring would you put more emphasis on education or experience?

Because I hire designers, I put more emphasis on thinking. I need people who are synthesis thinkers. People, who take the world around them and try to figure out how to apply it to games. If I had to say I have any bias, it's toward designers who have a bit more technical skills, some basic scripting, art tools and the like.

Do you have any final thoughts for people hoping to become a design director in the games industry?

Yes...

First: Play games. I don't mean computer games. I assume if you want to be a designer in the industry you already play a ton of computer games. I need my designers to have played all sorts of games. Play scrabble with your grandmother, play jacks with your little cousin, go to a playground, throw a ball out and watch what happens. Design is all about understanding how people interact with entertainment... and not just computer entertainment. I need designers who really enjoy figuring out how to make fun entertainment for people other than themselves!

Second: Join the IGDA, join the SIG that applies to you, volunteer, volunteer and volunteer!

So you feel that classic games still have their place to play in the industry, something like that is easy to overlook. Are there other pitfalls that people should look out for when starting a design document?

There are many. There are several mistakes I see young designers make over and over again, but one of the big ones I see a lot of is designers not knowing or remembering who their audience is. I've seen many design pitches for Facebook games that are nothing more than traditional games crammed into a social site. This does not take their audience into consideration and is one of the biggest mistakes you can make.

With regards to actually working in the industry, what would you say is the best thing about your role?

Thinking up goofy stuff! No, seriously! When I was at SOE, I had to break up a fight between two of the designers on my design team who were arguing over whether or not players should be able to learn to speak Jawa, how cool is that?

That's pretty damn cool if I'm honest, but with everything there must be a downside with that in mind, what's the worst thing about your role?

Working on things that either:

1. Never make it into production or

2. Make it into production, but get killed. It's SO hard to put so much creative work into creating great entertainment, only to have it never be allowed to entertain anyone.

So what's an average day for a Design Director like?

That sort of depends on what stage of the project you're in. If you're in pre-production then the sky's the limit. You mostly are either in design meetings where you brainstorm all sorts of insanity for the game or sitting at your desk writing documents that try to capture all the crazy stuff you came up with in the meetings

If you're in production, then you are heads down working with the tools to create the game. You may be level building, writing quests or you may be working with the programmer and artists answering questions: "No, the player should not be able to get up on the porch." "Yes, that car should be able to go up hills like that."

If you're in post production, you will likely be writing up a post-mortem, packing up/pulling together documentation for archives, working on final clean up, etc.

When you're brainstorming ideas, do you ever feel held back by technology or are we now at a stage where if you can imagine it we can do it?

I don't think I've ever felt really held back by technology. I've always been able to fit what I wanted to do into the technology of the day. In fact, that's one of the fun challenges, using what tools you have at hand to make the best game you possibly can.

Do you have any tips for surviving crunch?

Remember your family comes first. No one ever had "Wish I'd stayed at the office longer" written on their tombstone. Get sleep when you can and try REALLY hard to stay away from the awful snacks they will bring in!

So what are the longest hours you've worked during a crunch?

24+ … many nights spent sleeping under my desk.

How do you feel about the challenges women face in the industry?

They are there. I get very annoyed with people who think they aren't. There are explicit challenges (lack of female representation in the work force, female representation in games, etc.) and there are implicit problems, (the sentiment that a female on a team will "ruin their fun", the derision of female viewpoint, the perpetuation of the "locker room" culture, etc.) Both types are difficult to deal with, particularly as a lone female on a team. The solution has to be an industry wide one.

Do you think attitudes to women are changing in the industry?

Yes. They haven't moved as quickly as I would like, but they certainly are. The overwhelming success of the "social games" has brought the spotlight right on to the female gamer and, by association, the female game developer as something desirable to have on the team.

Do you feel women need to work harder to prove themselves in the industry?

At this point, yes. As the old saying goes, "Everything Fred Astaire did, Ginger Rogers did backwards and in high heels." There is quite a bit of truth to that. We must regularly prove that we can "make traditional games."

If you could offer one piece of advice to someone starting out in the industry what would that be?

Never give up. Never surrender. Truthfully, if you want to be in this industry, you have to fight for it. You have to continue to be on top of your game, on top of your network and be able to keep up with some of the most brilliantly creative people you'll ever meet. There will always be new people hounding your heels or obstacles thrown in your way. You can NOT give up and you can NOT surrender!

If you could change one thing about the industry what would that be?

That's a tough one. On an industry level, if I could wave a wand I'd make sure all companies saw the value in training their managers. Most of the developers are great at developing, but have had no experience with managing people. It's a skill that must be learned and trying to learn it while heading a multimillion dollar title is just bad.

On a personal level, I'd really like to see some of the lingering prejudices fade away. We still run into problems with minorities getting into the industry and, once there, getting promoted. I'd like to see more minorities being given opportunities to speak at conferences, being given leadership roles on titles and promotions into executive slots. The good news about that one is we are making progress!

Name:	Sophie Blackmore	**Currently working for:**	Rockstar
Age:	34	**Current role:**	Senior Designer
Sex:	Female	**Length of Service:**	5 months

Sophie was introduced to me via my good friend Darren. A talented designer she was more than willing to help with this book.

Why did you want to get into the games industry?

I've always been a gamer since my father brought home an Amstrad CPC-464, way back in the 80s, on which I played classics such as Harrier Attack and Digger. I used to play the arcade machines at the local burger joint, spending all my saved-up lunch money on trying to get my name in the High Score tables. Although I studied Religious Studies at university, I kept up my gaming, becoming known as the Queen of Goldeneye among my peers. My flatmates and I would stay up for hours playing Puzzle Bobble on the N64, I split my time evenly between studying for my degree and improving my gaming skills.

How long have you worked in the industry?

13 years. I'm pretty much an industry veteran!

Who have you worked for in the industry?

The most notable names would be The Creative Assembly (creators of the Total War franchise), SEGA, Kuju, but I've also worked for Black Cactus, Mind's Eye, nDreams, Ideaworks 3D, many more.

What do you do in the industry?

As a game designer I'm responsible for all aspects of the game, from initial concept document through to the Game Design Document and post-production. This includes tasks such as narrative, level design, player character and A.I. design, UI flow, sfx, game mechanics, marketing and much, much more. I love the diversity that the job offers, from one day to the next I'll be doing completely different tasks, so I never get bored.

What would you say is the highlight of your career so far?

I got to attend E3 in 2006 to promote Spartan: Total Warrior which included meeting lots of booth babes.

We haven't looked at booth babes in the industry, but we have spoken about some of the perceived challenges women may face in the industry. Do you think that booth babes are a negative reflection on the industry or is it more a "sex sells" concept?

I think when I first joined the industry I was quite a militant feminist and found the idea of women "being take advantage of" quite distasteful. I've always been the only female in the smaller companies I've worked for, so found the male-dominated workspace pretty intimidating, posters of bikini-clad models adorning the walls. However, after a few years I learnt to accept a few things, blokes will be blokes; women have attractive figures and there's nothing wrong with appreciating that. I also realised that the booth babes I encountered were fun-loving, happy-go-lucky girls, who were simply doing a job (a well-paid job!) and enjoying it. Getting hover-hugged by random sweaty geeks might not be everyone's idea of fun, but it's pretty empowering and quite a laugh. I got special treatment as I was pretty much the only girl having my photos taken with them.

So what would you consider the lowlight of your career so far?

Being stuck in short-term contract roles for a couple of years. You can't properly get your teeth into a role if it's only short term, you never know where the next paycheque is coming from.

We discussed the nature of temp roles in the industry earlier on. Do you feel that more companies are heading in this direction?

In the last few years I have definitely seen a trend towards only employing people on short term contracts. I imagine it's to do with the economical climate, coupled with the rise of bedroom developers (directly influenced by the accessibility of iOS and other platforms). It's great that your average coder/designer can set up their own company and get a game out on the app. store these days, but on the other hand it does mean those of us who want full-time permanent positions in good companies are at a disadvantage.

How did you originally get into the industry and did you do anything unique to increase your chances?

When my degree ended I faced the choice of becoming a teacher or applying for a Q.A. job. I applied for both positions and was offered both. My gut instinct was to go for the career which provided the most fun, so I accepted the Q.A. position and have never looked back. Q.A. is a great first stepping stone to get into the industry, as you get a taste of how both developers and publishers work, from there you can decide where you want to take your career.

How did you get into your current role?

During my time in Q.A., I had a tendency to try to improve the game mechanics of the games I tested. Unfortunately, as a tester your ideas rarely get heard over all the devs. and other people above you, which I found rather frustrating. I realised I had a flair for the creative side of the development process, so after about a year and a half in Q.A. I applied for a Junior Game Designer position in Oxford at Exient Entertainment. From there I just kept up my passion for design, progressed through the design path, from Junior to Game Designer, to Experienced and then Senior Designer.

What advice would you give to people looking to be a senior designer in the industry?

Everyone sees game design as a "cool" career where you get to make and play games. It certainly does have its awesome moments, but bear in mind it is just a job, that there will be dull days, impossible tasks, crunch time where you work till midnight for weeks at a time. It's a career you have to love right from the start, or you'll quickly tire of it. These days you can do Game Design courses at University, though I believe hands-on experience will always look better on your C.V. Try to get an unpaid intern role or apply for work experience at developers to get a taste of the role.

So do you feel a career in the games industry is glamorised to an extent?

There is definitely a glamorisation of a games industry career. We do long working hours for far less pay than the equivalent position in non-games companies, but to a certain extent you could say that about any supposedly "glamorous" career e.g. modelling, the entertainment industry, and pole-dancing. I'm sure they're all great at times and have their obvious perks, but I think just like any career, every job will have its downsides and drawbacks.

If hiring, would you put more emphasis on education or experience?

It depends on the role. At The Creative Assembly the designers tended to have degrees in subjects relevant to the Total War franchise i.e. History, English, Politics, etc. However, personally I think experience is really important to fully understanding what will be expected of you in your career. You need to see the ups and downs of game design and the only way to do that is to get involved as early as possible.

Do you have any final thoughts for people hoping to become a senior game designer in the games industry?

Don't think that it's all fun and games! It is mainly fun and games, but it tends to be a case of work hard, play hard. Every step of the way you'll be expected to prove yourself and your game ideas.

With regards to actually working in the industry, what would you say is the best thing about your role?

Seeing aspects of your design going into the game and when it's released thinking "I made that!"

What's the worst thing about your role?

Crunch time!!
You might be working 14 hour days for weeks at a time. Most game developers make you sign out of the European Working Time Directive. Some people in the industry think that a well-organised project should never go into crunch, but it's more a case of making sure the game is the best it can be by putting in the extra effort to polish and tweak it.

One thing I didn't expect starting this book was the completely opposite reactions some people have to crunch. I've always seen it as part of the job, do you feel the same or do you feel with our ability to now patch titles and the surge in mobile and social games that crunch may become a thing of the past?

I've always believed that a well-organised company with hard-working employees should never have to do crunch times and to a certain extent, I've seen this proven by most of the companies I've worked at. However, if it is needed to make the game you're working on the best it can be, then you should do it without (too much) complaining. Again, in many other industries unpaid overtime is simply a part of the job. I've a friend in banking that routinely has to work entire weekends without compensation, though her salary probably makes up for her lost time, unlike those in the games industry. Basically, you've got to be passionate about your job and love what you're doing, whether you're working on the next triple A, chart-topping, next-gen. console game, or a branded social game for Facebook. You can't be half-hearted about a career in the games industry.

Do you have any tips for surviving crunch?

Ha! Focus on the end goal. If you crunch hard, the product will be that much better when it hits the shelves. Don't be tempted to pig out on the free pizza and food deliveries you get given, bring in your own healthy food too. Your brain can't work properly on E numbers, additives and monosodium glutamate. Try to do some exercise, even if it is approaching midnight and dark outside, go for a walk round the block. Make sure you stay friendly with your teammates, being locked in an office with them for 14 hours a day can almost bring you to blows, so keep it friendly and take regular breaks to play fun games such as Rock Band and Singstar. Oh and make sure you shower, there's nothing worse than the smell of stinky developers mingling with old pizza, cigarettes and coffee.

Sounds lovely, let's move on. What are the longest hours you've worked during a crunch?

I think I've been fairly lucky, my worst crunch time was way back in Q.A. when I was working from 10a.m. – 1a.m. for a couple of weeks at a time. It could have been a lot worse; many of my mates have done all-nighters and then carried on into the next day.

So what's an average day for a senior games designer like?

It's always varied and interesting. One day you might be doing a pitch document to send out to publishers and C.E.Os (in which case you have to "dumb down" the terminology to a certain extent); the next day you might be placing weapon pickups across a level, triggering sfx "stings", designing NPC combat systems, naming your characters and the world they live in or even attending press days and conferences to speak about your games. This is why I love the role, there's such a variety of tasks involved.

How do you feel about the challenges women face in the industry?

I'm not sure there are any challenges that men in the industry wouldn't face. Perhaps women designers have to work a little harder to prove they know what they're talking about and that they're as passionate about games and gaming as men, but a quick death-match in Quake or COD or BF will usually sort out any doubters. I used to get offended by some guys just dismissing certain game play ideas and took it really personally, but then I realised they do that to each other as well, that they weren't victimising me for being a girl in the industry. Perhaps the biggest challenge (which I overcame with gusto) is the amount of swearing and general blokeish behaviour you encounter. If you can't beat them, join them.

Do you think attitudes to women are changing in the industry?

I'm not sure. It takes a certain type of person to join the industry, regardless of gender. I think those who think they're being discriminated against just need to realise that's how the industry works, it can be a harsh mistress, but you get out what you put in.

Do you feel women need to work harder to prove themselves in the industry?

To a certain extent, yes, but in my experience this only seems to be an initial problem. Once you've demonstrated you're just the same as the guys in terms of gaming prowess, knowledge and skills, you can actually go further than they might.

If you could offer one piece of advice to someone starting out in the industry what would that be?

Don't be afraid to ask your peers for help or advice. You might end up getting some of your best inspiration from unexpected corners. Just make sure you credit them!

Name:	Will Luton	Currently working for:	Mobile Pie
Age:	27	Current role:	Creative Director
Sex:	Male	Length of Service:	2 Years

Will was a tester who I worked with at SEGA, it was his first role in the industry. An ambitious young guy, in his short career Will has already become a creative director for Mobile Pie and regularly features in Develop magazine.

Why did you want to get into the games industry?

Because I loved games and had this feeling that they weren't everything they could be. I wanted games that were different. I'm still working out what that is.

How long have you worked in the industry?

Since 2008, so three years.

Who have you worked for in the industry?

Mobile Pie and SEGA Europe before that and some retail work.

What do you do in the industry?

We're a small company, so I do lots of things. I oversee the creative process and define the design of all our own IP, but also seek new business, talk at conferences, write and generally get the company name out there. We have very good recognition in the industry considering our size and how long we've been around.

What would you say is the highlight of your career so far?

I've had several. First job and moving from Q.A. to Production very quickly were great moments, as was being asked to write for Develop and Pocket Gamer, being in Edge magazine and speaking at some big conferences like Develop and the Mobile Games Forum. Also seeing great reviews for games that have been your baby is an amazing buzz and meeting legends like Ian Livingston. However, I would say that last year getting named by Develop magazine as one of their 30 under 30 (30 people under 30 years old to watch in the industry) was momentous. I'm very proud of that.

I must admit I was quite pleased seeing you in the 30 under 30. How does it feel to be someone who Develop suggests we should look out for?

It feels great. I'm really proud of it. I'd become aware of the award the year before and knew I wanted to be in it by the next year, it had become a goal. So when nominations came I dropped some massive hints to get nominated which someone obviously did.

So what would you consider the lowlight of your career so far?

I delivered a talk I was nervous about, had not properly prepared for and totally messed it up in front of lots of industry luminaries. That was embarrassing, but I actually got lots of praise and it was great for the company so I see it as a positive. That sort of thing will no doubt happen to you if you're ambitious and it's a huge learning experience, so embrace it.

I'm pushed for a real lowlight, but there were times when I started out, doing Q.A. that I felt very frustrated doing low-level repetitive work. I've always been very ambitious and so I used that frustrated energy to make something happen and managed to move on to a production team. For a few months however it felt like hell and I was very sulky.

Thanks Will that's quite a lot to have achieved in such a short space of time. How did you originally get into the industry?

I was studying Physics at university, trying to work out how to use it to get in to the industry without being a programmer when I was reading Edge and saw an advert for a games design course at Salford Uni. I dropped out and started at Huddersfield University's B.A. (Hons) Computer Games Design, which was rubbish, but part of it was a year in industry. Most people didn't get placements, but I was adamant I was going to do something amazing. I sent off two letters, one was to a H.R. person I'd met at a studio and the other was just to the H.R. department at SEGA Europe with this covering letter about how, as young boy, I'd dreamed of working for SEGA. SEGA called me in, interviewed me and offered me a 12 month placement. I was very excited.

That must have been an exciting offer to get. Did you get paid for your placement or was it volunteer work?

It was paid, but I wouldn't have been able to live without the student loan, which I received at half rate as part of a placement. Also, when I went from Q.A. to production, I stayed on the same hourly wage and as there wasn't overtime I took a real hit. It was difficult to live for a while, but that's the hardship of your first steps in.

How did you get into your current role?

After a few months of Q.A. I became really frustrated. I begged and pleaded my way in to Product Development and became an Assistant Producer, it was suggested that I could stay in the job, but I decided to go back to finish university. I kept up good links with SEGA throughout the course and was expecting to go back there as I was tipped off a cool job was coming up, but just before I graduated I was told about a company that had started up in my home town of Bristol. I got in contact with the founders, Rich and Tom, did a week's trial, the job at SEGA never did materialize and so I became Mobile Pie's first employee. Recently I was invited to the board, which was an honour. I never intended to work in mobile, but I'm glad I did. It's a much more exciting place to be at than a big corporate company focusing on shrinking retail and I've managed to achieve a level of notoriety I wouldn't have done in a larger company.

So would you say small companies have greater opportunities?

Small companies do have greater opportunities, if they're growing and becoming successful. You can rise up really quickly, which is much harder in an established company, but lots of small start ups fail rather quickly, so you could be out of a job rather quickly. My advice would be look for a one or two man show that are starting to get noticed and get in contact. Showing you're interested in what they do, their games and saying you want to work with them makes you a strong candidate if and when they begin recruiting. Also, small companies are more fun as you feel you have more input, rather than being a small cog in a large machine.

What advice would you give to people looking to be a creative director in the industry?

To go anywhere in the industry, or any industry, I'd give the same advice: Be confident, make friends, ask questions and learn. Tell people what you want to achieve and ask them to help you. They almost definitely will. Even go as far as being pushy to get what you want, but don't be a dick. It goes both ways, so help them and remember that you don't know everything, so don't pretend to. Don't be horrible to people and don't burn bridges. Always work towards the best solution for the team and the project, not your ego. But most of all be honest, ignore negativity and enjoy what you do.

If hiring would you put more emphasis on education or experience?

Either. It's whatever demonstrates you're capable of doing the job. What's more important for us in a small team is attitude and personality. Things like hobbies and volunteering are great things to have on a C.V. They separate you out as an interesting candidate and give you something to talk about in an interview.

Any final thoughts for people hoping to become a Creative Director in the games industry?

Believe in yourself and don't be afraid of contacting people and making friends. It can be who you know.

Good advice with regards to actually working in the industry. What would you say is the best thing about your role?

That I meet lots of cool people and make the things that I want to make.

I guess ultimately most people would love to be in the position of making what they want to make. Do you think there's a certain element of luck to get to that position or with determination can anyone do it?

It's absolutely not about luck. I put my humble successes down to knowing what I want, asking for it and working hard towards it. You will get opportunities in your career which, if you make the most of, some people will see as luck. But it's not. It's a lot to do with attitude. How you think about what you want and how you interact with others. Have an ego, be ambitious, but keep it in check and make sure you pay everyone around you the respect they deserve. That will lead to great, positive responses to you. Nobody gets anywhere by shouting and being arrogant, those people stay at the bottom of the pile.

What's the worst thing about your role?

Sometimes it is knuckling down and hammering out something mundane, but that's just work, right?

Sadly, you're right Will. No matter how much fun any industry is we all have paperwork, so what's an average day for a creative director like?

It varies. One day might be travelling out to a conference. Another day I could be writing a script about a professor and sassy robot. Then recording voices, designing business cards or being asked what your average day is. It's so varied, but as we get bigger it's more and more admin or writing tasks.

Do you have any tips for surviving crunch?

Don't do it! Seriously!

If you feel like the amount of work you're asked to do needs a "survival tactic" then say "no". You shouldn't be making yourself ill or putting your social life and relationships at risk for your job. You'll get further by going home at a reasonable hour, getting some rest and sleep than crunching through and being ill, tired and angry.

So what are the longest hours you've worked during a crunch?

I worked the odd weekend. I often avoided it. It's not a reality of the industry and it shouldn't be a badge of honour.

How do you feel about the challenges women face in the industry?

I think there's a real drought of qualified women in the industry and those wanting to take their first steps in, which means that many companies are very, unintentionally, male orientated, Mobile Pie included. That obviously makes it difficult for women to feel comfortable making games their career path.

Do you think attitudes to women are changing in the industry?

I think that there are some people with very poor attitudes to women in this industry. Mostly they're old dragons making games with big explosions for teenage boys and are dying out. Our gender split for a recent game was 62% female to 38% male, so I think it's already changed.

If you could offer one piece of advice to someone starting out in the industry what would that be?

Get out and do. Be involved in everything. Talk to everyone.

Thanks a lot Will it's been great catching up.

Name:	Jez Harris	***Currently working for:***	Supermassive Games
Age:	32	***Current role:***	Production Manager
Sex:	Male	***Length of Service:***	8 Months

Jez and I met while working on a career advice panel for the Eurogamer Expo. He's one of those guys you meet in the industry that you've worked with on many projects without ever actually meeting. He was keen to offer some advice and answer a few questions.

Why did you want to get into the games industry?

There are a handful of defining moments which ultimately brought me to it, but the groundwork was laid by friends with NESs and C64s and my first Gameboy. Though I was relatively academic (at least until 16 or so at any rate) and sporty, a love of games was consistent throughout my childhood, it took until I was 18 to definitively decide I wanted to make a career of games. Looking back, it was the only thing I ever saw myself doing professionally, regardless of how likely I may have perceived that to be at the time.

How long have you worked in the industry?

Around 13 and half years. I started aged 18 in Bullfrog's Q.A. department back in 1998.

Who have you worked for in the industry?

I began as a tester with Bullfrog (/EA). I'm enormously grateful to have been given the opportunity and I loved a huge amount of the 12 months I spent there, but Q.A. wasn't ultimately for me. I'm sympathetic now to the guys in test who focus far too much energy on giving 'design feedback' rather than finding bugs. It's not what they really should be doing and a lot of developers can get irrationally irritated by it, but that's what I did. As someone who actually wanted to get into design or production, it worked in my favour as my ways brought me into contact with more senior staff I would otherwise never have encountered. Through those unexpected connections, with a headcount freeze on at EA, I landed a junior design position with the now defunct Hothouse Creations in Bristol. After two years there, the bulk of which was spent designing the levels for Gangsters 2, an opportunity arose to head back to EA and join the Harry Potter team as a designer.

Four years and maybe five shipped titles (including a couple of non-Potters in the form of Catwoman and Battlefield: Modern Combat) later, I was offered the position of Lead Designer at Relentless Software in Brighton, on the Buzz! series for SCEE. Five titles in three and a half years this time, including my first credits as External Producer and it was time for another move.

Two release-free stints at Headstrong and UTV Ignition as Senior Designer, Design Manager and latterly Producer, preceded settling into where you now find me, Production Manager at Supermassive Games. So in summary, Bullfrog/EA, Hothouse Creations, EA, Relentless, Headstrong/Kuju, UTV Ignition and Supermassive Games

Do you have any preference between working for a publisher or a developer?

I've not actually worked in the publishing arm of a publisher, internal and external development, yes, publishing, no. The role of external producer (where we'd subcontracted other developers, but weren't actually the publisher) was one I absolutely enjoyed. Getting out of the office, working with new people you're *not* accustomed to seeing daily, representing the best interests of your employer, all terrific. At that point I'd not done any internal production officially, but I now have - and I do think (though I have to say this, it's true) I get more out of it. The direct exposure to and involvement with the creative remains critical to my love of the business. It's not that you don't or can't have that in an external production or publisher-side position, but from my experience it's certainly diminished.

What do you do in the industry?

What I do now is the role of Production Manager, which is for the most part what most studios would refer to as a Producer.

What would you say is the highlight of your career so far?

I don't mean this in an arrogant way, but there are lots! That shouldn't be too surprising after 13 years in the industry, but it's nice to reflect and know that it has been, continues to be, a consistently interesting career.

Giving my first public lecture, which I was stunned to find was attended by a couple of hundred people. Being invited to join BAFTA, amazing trips to Euro Disney, Tunisia, E3, IFA, GDC (with EA and Relentless). Shipping my first title with a Lead Designer credit

(Buzz! The Mega Quiz) and getting a 9/10 Eurogamer review for it. Helping to save a studio, albeit only temporarily, from imminent closure and though it may sound convenient to say it, most recently finding myself working on a potentially huge title, after doubting myself for a couple of years on non-projects.

So what would you consider the lowlight of your career so far?

A couple of poor career moves. The first was an innocent mistake as the motivation for moving, location primarily, wasn't really sufficient (you should always go for projects and people first). It also turned out that I was as wrong for them as they were for me. I left after 7 months or so with barely a goodbye. With redundancy looming there, a sharpish exit had been required and out of necessity, convenience and, to be fair, some ill-judged good feelings I spent 18 months at a studio initially in transition, soon after on the brink and later closed. To have played a significant part in preventing its closure, salvaging 25 jobs in the process, only to have it shut down 8 months later on questionable grounds was hard, although it's fair to say I learnt an awful lot. The upside being the relief of joining a smartly run studio with standout projects again, a phenomenal state change.

How did you originally get into the industry and did you do anything unique to increase your chances?

The potted version:
I looked up EA's number
I got put through to Bullfrog's H.R. department
I got an interview
I got the job

This was straight out of sixth form (near enough anyway. I'd spent a few months perilously close to allowing my Saturday job to become permanent), EA was the first company I called. I did have some 'notable' experience on my C.V., I'd attended an EA focus group when I was 14 or so, which was a talking point. I'd won my school's GCSE Design prize for a project on a new Megadrive controller. My A-Level Design coursework included an interview I'd conducted with the then deputy editor of Sega Saturn Magazine, Matt Yeo, but for all intents and purposes I was simply a keen kid looking for a job in Q.A., I got one. What I did once I had it got me to where I am now.

I've assumed for the last few years that the way in which I got into the business was no longer relevant, that the industry had grown up too much for tales of such innocuous beginnings to still be useful, practical advice. I think however that's nonsense, although there might in some cases be more hoops to jump though these days, there are in fact far more opportunities than ever before for young, talented people wanting to make games. The difference, if there is one, is that someone like me back then would probably struggle now due to a lack of demonstrable skills, with the tools that we have freely available now there'd be no excuse for that.

Do you think it is much harder now to get in the industry than it once was?

I honestly don't think it's harder as such. Though I don't of course have first-hand experience of breaking into the business of late, I think the immeasurably wider composition of it means there are far more opportunities. What I would reiterate is that it's likely more difficult for someone with no demonstrable skills to get in these days because there's no excuse for not having something in your back pocket to prove your worth. There's a lot of derision, some misplaced, some not, of university 'games' courses, but they're an example of what's there for people now which wasn't there 15 years ago. The wealth of free 'game-making' tools, be it Little Big Planet, UDK or SketchUp, is another. It's easier (and therefore harder, all at the same time) to prove your worth now than ever before, so make sure you do.

Don't expect to get in on the back of a Saturday job in GAME, an 'extensive knowledge of games' (believe me, there is always someone who knows an awful lot more) and a smile, **do something**. Make something, draw something, plan something, anything to prove you've got the talent and, crucially, the motivation. Most studios are crying out for exciting young talent, so show that's what you are in all your dealings with them.

How did you get into your current role?

Ignoring the merits (or lack thereof) of my C.V., contacts and networking. Specifically, having been invited to an awards dinner by a recruitment agency I'd recently done business with, I bumped into the guys from Supermassive, the senior management of which I'd worked with in various studios over the years and with whom I'd always maintained good relations, got chatting. A fortnight or so later I started here.
It's not just about contacts though, of course. Whilst I haven't always delivered or lived up to my potential and there are certainly a few characters out there who'd agree with me wholeheartedly on that, I have spent well over a decade doing what I do, for the

most part reasonably well and with a smile on my face. Any job I get now or in the future will in some way have been affected by that.

We speak a fair bit about networking in the book. Do you have any advice on how people can get the ball rolling and begin building up their network without having worked in the industry?

Another that comes down to a huge amount of motivation. There are opportunities. Even simply contacting a games studio, 90% of your mails will never get a response, but give someone a reason to respond, hope it finds its way to a good 'un and you might just get something out of it. Attend shows and events. BAFTA and the Eurogamer Expo are just two that do a hell of a lot to present keen folk with the chance to talk to developers. This is a tactic that can work. An example: There's a guy who came to hear me talk at the EG Expo two years running. He'd never worked in games, he was just finishing university on the second occasion, but I've now tried to hire him three times. I'll get him one day, but the point is, he was a clear talent, had something to say and show for himself and he's already a success. The flipside of course is the number of people you meet at such events who really have very little more to say than "I want to work in games because I like them". That's a start certainly, but try and have a little more up your sleeve than that. Impress someone in the industry when you get the chance to meet them and good things may happen. If that sounds like too much bother, you'll need to find another avenue to pursue.

What advice would you give to people looking to be a Production Manager in the industry?

Do something else first! If a Producer's doing their job well, they're facilitating and organizing a team, however large or small, of likely hugely gifted people who know how to do their jobs. Having some understanding of what those jobs entail and what's required to actually make a video game is crucial. I'd suggest the only way to get that understanding is to have done some of it yourself or, at the very least, to have been around people making games for quite some time and there aren't many ways of doing that without being one of the people making them. What you shouldn't do is look for a role such as mine expecting it to mean that you're in charge as that's not the way it works. Whilst it is my dubious honour to be reminding people of when they need to have things ready by, indeed defining in some instances what those things need to be, the real purpose of the role is to ensure that those people have the facility to deliver those things, to be able to do what they do to the best of their ability. It's a question of being an asset and resource juggler, not a dictator.

If hiring would you put more emphasis on education or experience?

Experience, but not necessarily years on the clock.

Do you have any final thoughts for people hoping to become a Production Manager in the games industry?

I'd find it hard to understand someone who wanted to make games wanting to be a Producer from day one. If you do though, you're going to need to learn all you can about all aspects of game creation. One of the most repeated complaints people have with producers is that they don't know what they're doing and that's more commonly true than it should be! You're there to help people get their job done, don't make it about you.

With regards to actually working in the industry, what would you say is the best thing about your role?

Seeing a great game come together. It's a privileged position to be in as I get to see all the component pieces fall into place. Some on the team need to be so focused on their own particular workload they find it impossible to see the bigger picture until it's done. I get to consistently see how fantastic everyone's work is which makes keeping myself motivated through to the end of the project, something some can find difficult, extremely easy.

What's the worst thing about your role?

Maintaining an objective view and keeping one's eye on that bigger picture takes some effort. It's the nature of the business for us to have tight schedules and budgets and being the person who has to say something's good enough, it's time to move on or it's not good enough, it's going to have to go, to the guys who've put it together isn't ever especially nice. The very worst thing, mind, is seeing a project you love lose its funding and get cancelled. Thankfully I've not yet seen that from this position, but having seen it as a designer I'd fully expect it to be even harder now.

So what's an average day for a Production Manager like?

Cliché, but I'm really not sure there is such a thing as an average day. It's all about reacting to the needs of the project at any given time and as every project and team is different, so too are those needs. However, there are of course some consistencies, which might include attending one or more of the daily scrum meetings; doing a build review and distributing feedback and specific tasks based on it; liaising with the publisher about any outstanding issues or upcoming milestones; catching up with the EP and Game Director on problems and priorities; orchestrating the commission and distribution of any outsourced artwork and one too many cigarette breaks.

Do you have any tips for surviving crunch?

With a couple of exceptions, it's really not something I've experienced profoundly. If there's a tip from me, it would be to aim to work in well managed studios. There are more of them out there than some would lead you to believe.

So what are the longest hours you've worked during a crunch?

Q.A., weekends, one or two all-nighters getting Dungeon Keeper 2 finished. Sporadic weekend and late night work, but rarely extensive or over prolonged periods.

There was something charming or at the least compelling about those long hours as a young man. When I was in Q.A. most of my friends were still at school or had just started university, being in a job that required that extra dedication seemed genuinely 'cool'. That it was making video games made it all the more so. That was the reality, I enjoyed it. No one was exploiting anyone or if they were surely the enthusiasm and consent of the alleged 'exploited' precludes it from being exploitation? That may be an appallingly naïve view limited solely to the exploitation of young, underpaid and over-enthusiastic game testers. There are stories, of course, of awful personal problems, ill-health; failed relationships, caused by 'crunch', but it's simply not something of which I've had first-hand experience.

If you could change one thing about the industry what would that be?

My answer to this would be different on any given day, but I'll give you two.

Its public face. As a business we're crap at self-promotion. The answer to that is not to have a huge marketing and P.R. department doing the front of house stuff for us. The creatives should do more, be allowed to do more, to champion their efforts. It's not a completely fair parallel, but you wouldn't see Amblin's P.R. guy on Jonathan Ross promoting Spielberg's new film, you'd see Spielberg. Some are getting there, the Naughty Dog boys get some great mainstream coverage in the States and I can see the likes of Jenova Chen becoming a 'face' There are of course some issues (why should individuals take the limelight for such a fundamentally team-driven effort?), but overall we should at least be making more effort with it. I'll settle for Will Byles appearing on The Review Show as a starting point.

From a development perspective, I'd dearly love to figure out a way of standardising the creation of games. Due to ever changing technology it's unlikely to happen and in many respects the ever widening possibilities for what we'll be able to make are too exciting to want to see the back of, but part of what makes this business so challenging and often frustrating is that we're constantly re-inventing how we go about our work. There are some fundamentals of course, which are unlikely to change profoundly anytime soon and rightly so, but standardising tools and techniques, establishing a common language for the medium that would be positive in a lot of ways. Anyone can pick up a pen and write a story or grab a camera and point it at something to make a film, however crude, but the barrier to entry in making a game remains off-puttingly high.

How do you feel about the challenges women face in the industry?

I'm not sure I'm able to fully rationalise my feelings on the matter. It's a big subject and one that's arguably not limited to challenges within this particular business. It's a male-dominated industry, that much is obvious, but wishing to avoid sweeping generalisations I doubt this is the forum to get to the bottom of it. I would say that I've absolutely seen some of the problems women in development face, but then I've seen a lot of the problems that people in development face and I'm not totally convinced that many of them are gender-centric.

Do you think attitudes to women are changing in the industry?

As it grows up yes, of course. Lest we forget, this started as a geek industry (some would say it remains so), in the U.K. at least by boys in their bedrooms. Gaming for an awfully long time was a predominantly male pastime. The biggest titles, in our part of the business, remain targeted largely at lads, the GTAs, the CODs, the FIFAs. Video games shops continue to look and smell like teenage boys' bedrooms. It's not surprising that women still aren't too involved with it. However, 'the games industry' encompasses an awful lot more now than it did even 5 years ago, with both the traditional sector, Nintendo being the prime example, the new frontiers of iOS, Facebook and browsers offering an infinitely wider range of experiences in what gets played and how it's made. That fact alone means that antiquated attitudes to women, if they do remain, are increasingly irrelevant; there's just too much choice and opportunity there now for it to be an issue.

Do you feel women need to work harder to prove themselves in the industry?

I'll say simply that they shouldn't, I'm not aware of ever having seen evidence that they do.

Jez, it's been great catching up thanks for your time.

Name:	Aaron Yeung	**Currently working for:**	Doublesix
Age:	32	**Current role:**	Associate Producer
Sex:	Male	**Length of Service:**	3 Years

Aaron and I have found ourselves working together at two different companies. I've seen him go from testing to production. We started catching up by discussing his career so far.

Why did you want to get into the games industry?

I decided long ago (sorry for the song reference) that I didn't want to wake up at 30-40 asking myself why I was going to work. I wanted to work in an industry I was actually interested in and I love games and gaming, so it seemed perfect.

Do you feel that's been achieved?

To a point, yes. People's targets change as they near/complete previous targets. I'm happy in that I'm working in the industry but obviously I want to work on an AAA game at some point in my life.

How long have you worked in the industry?

4-5 years now I started at Sega in Q.A. and I moved to Kuju as a Corporate Production Assistant and now I'm working as an A.P.

Who have you worked for in the industry?

Sega, Kuju

As you have experience comprised of one studio and one publisher, where would you suggest someone starting out in the industry should aim for?

It's VERY difficult to say. Clearly it's very difficult to get into production, so you should really take what you can get. I would say that starting as a developer side producer is much better, as publisher production can't work without dev. production (but it can vice versa). Plus you get more pay and better benefits in publishing, but not as much creative input or team bonding.

What do you do in the industry?

Associate Producer – Scheduling, Office Management, P.R., Marketing, Submissions, Q.A. management, outsourcer communications, main contact for Sony, managing Work Experience, budgeting

How do you find managing the publisher/developer relationship on such complicated project(s)?

It's VERY difficult. There are various issues when dealing with either Sony or Microsoft or Steam which are all compounded when you have to juggle them together. I.e. for AZMD we need an Xbox Publisher in order to release it on Xbox. Microsoft have a policy of not allowing games to be released on their platforms if they were previously released on another platform without at least 60% additional content (although this is now being relaxed on 1 game I know of but cannot say, no, it's not one of our games). This makes it difficult to do exclusive content for other platforms without breaching Xbox rules and getting removed from the store.
Also, with Millionaire we have had LOADS of issues dealing with licensors etc. Getting approvals for all parties and trying to keep to a schedule is very difficult!

What would you say is the highlight of your career so far?

Being at PAX, seeing the public playing the game I have been working on and loving it!! Also, having my creative ideas actually put into the game!

So what would you consider the lowlight of your career so far?

Working at Sega. No seriously, basically because they treated me like crap, made me feel like the industry was a joke and almost made me hate the industry!! Spending an entire year worrying about not having a job next week was far from fun.

How did you originally get into the industry and did you do anything unique to increase your chances?

Initially a friend heard an advert for Sega Q.A. on the radio and told me about it. I was at university at the time so didn't really have time to do both. Completed university and applied for a role as FM08 tester. Got the job and started within the week. Not sure I did anything different there.

How did you get into your current role?

To get into Kuju I went to Eurogamer (Expo) and randomly spoke to someone. I had done a database type degree and this helped me get the job over others so was unique. Unfortunately that role has changed so others with the same background would not get that role now.

What advice would you give to people looking to be an A.P. in the industry?

This truly depends on their backgrounds. Many people wanting to do production are people who want to work in games, but have no technical knowledge (i.e. code or art) and therefore assume that's the only thing they can do (especially in a development environment). I would tend to agree here, although it is very useful to have a working knowledge of each discipline.

So to get in... For people yet to start university I would say study a project management type degree. This will get you a role as a project manager in a studio, one way of getting into production. I know that Sony and MS do these types of roles, but only really the larger studios can afford this type of role.

For those who have not gone to university or have already finished their studies they should try to get into Q.A. Any Q.A. at first, but I would recommend a small studio as you have more opportunity to progress within as well as being given responsibilities outside a normal Q.A. remit.

If hiring would you put more emphasis on education or experience?

Experience, games development cannot be learnt. It is constantly changing and nothing you learn at university can compare to hands on experience

So would you say there's little to no worth in studying?

That's my personal opinion, unless you are doing code. There's nothing that you can't show in a portfolio or through experience that a degree gives you. Artists can learn techniques at home and spend more time on the best software to make their portfolios. Harder to relate this "rule" to production as it's kind of an ad-hoc role and there's nothing really (apart from learning scrum techniques) that you can learn to prepare yourself. There's no degree in computer game development that actually give direct experience in development.

If you could change one thing in the industry what would it be?

Hmmm... I have a couple of options here... you choose:

1 - Too many people don't realise how lucky they are to be:

a) Working in a job they enjoy and

b) In an industry that is so relaxed. I think this leads to a lot of people becoming disillusioned with how things are run, when they start off with almost utopian ideas of how games are made.

2 – Reviewers. Seriously what's the point? There's so much wrong with this section of the industry (and not just for gaming!) you get a 10-20 hour game, play maybe an hour of it and make assumptions on the rest without seeing most of the game. Even if they standardized the rating system (i.e. everyone knows 7 in Edge is high).
Rant over.

Do you have any final thoughts for people hoping to become an A.P. in the games industry?

A couple:

- Don't expect to have it easy. The producer is the last person to get thanks when things go well, the first person to get it in the neck when things go wrong.

- It's VERY hard to get into. The only roles I know that lead directly into a full producer role are Associate Producers and Project Managers. A.P. roles are very difficult to find (especially without experience). The same can be said for project manager roles, which only really appear in larger corporations.

With regards to actually working in the industry, what would you say is the best thing about your role?

Being involved in lots of different things. I'm not coding or drawing all the time. Each day is different.

What's the worst thing about your role?

All my deadlines come together. My work loads are either not enough or LOADS!! Nothing in between. Also there are constant ad hoc tasks. I must state this is due to being in a small studio. In a bigger organization this wouldn't happen, but that's the benefit of working in a smaller place

So what's an average day for an A.P. like?

See above. There is no "average day". Over the last couple of weeks I have been managing localization and ensuring text files are up-to-date and correct. Next weekend I have another convention to exhibit at...

Do you have any tips for surviving crunch?

Don't do it! ☺

I certainly feel a well managed crunch period can enhance the final quality of a game. Do you feel there's any worth in crunch at all?

In an ideal situation crunch should not be necessary. Schedules are made and these estimates should be relatively accurate. However, we all know that to be unrealistic. Crunch should be done when and if needed (i.e. to meet a submission deadline). If you are crunching for long periods of time it implies that something was wrong with the scheduling and planning part. Crunch is the bane of the industry, but it is essential. People should expect to have to crunch and be happy when they don't need to do it, not the other way around. If the estimates are coming from the team and they fall behind it's their responsibility to fix that.

So what are the longest hours you've worked during a crunch?

I did a double shift at Sega once working on The Golden Compass. What a waste of time that was!! Clear example that crunch is not always useful.

How do you feel about the challenges women face in the industry?

Challenges? The only challenges they have are that they have to learn to deal with geeks on a daily basis. It's not like other industries where they are pushed out. I know plenty of people who would happily hire a woman if she were the best or one of the better candidates.

Do you think attitudes to women are changing in the industry?

I think it's more to do with the attitudes of women to gaming rather than vice versa. The majority of women still see games as being for children.

Do you feel women need to work harder to prove themselves in the industry?

There aren't enough to make this statement worthwhile, at least on the dev. side. You could ask the same for men in P.R.

If you could offer one piece of advice to someone starting out in the industry what would that be?

Don't assume that you are the be all and end all of all gaming knowledge. There are always people who will know more or different things than you. Also be prepared to not earn as much money as your friends in similar roles in different industries.

Thanks for your time it's always good to see what you've been up to since we last worked together.

Name:	Paul Sedgmore	Currently working for:	Colossal Games
Age:	27	Current role:	Q.A. Manager
Sex:	Male	Length of Service:	6 Years

Paul also used to test for me at SEGA. A dedicated hard working member of the team it was good to see him now managing his own team.

Why did you want to get into the games industry?

Games have always been a huge passion of mine with some of my earliest memories being playing games with my dad on a Commodore 64 that he brought home one day. Being something that I have always enjoyed I was always intent on making a career of it.

How long have you worked in the industry?

I've worked in the industry for about 6 years now spread between publishers, development teams and helping friends with their Indie projects.

Who have you worked for in the industry?

So far I have worked for SEGA Europe Ltd which gave me the opportunity to work with development teams all over the world, Black Rock Studio and Colossal Games which is a start-up company currently working on our first title.

Do you have any preference, publisher or developer?

Both publishers and developers have positives, for example working at a publisher will get you a lot of varied experience very quickly due to the fact that they generally have a lot more product passing through their doors whereas working for a developer you have a lot more input into the game. My personal preference is working for developers as I find having direct access to the team makes getting the bugs fixed easier.

What do you do in the industry?

My job is to break the game and make accurate records of how it was done so that the development team can fix the issue. Sometimes this is easy as the bug will happen naturally, but then sometimes you have to really think about how you are going to force the game to break. We also have to make sure that the game meets the requirements that the platform holders set for titles to go onto their systems.

What would you say is the highlight of your career so far?

The highlight of my career is without a doubt getting the first game I was lead on past submission and into shops. There is nothing like the feeling you get from getting the game you put so much time and effort into the hands of the public.

So what would you consider the lowlight of your career so far?

The lowlight of my career has to be being made redundant from the job I had been doing for five years. It's always hard when you lose your job, but when you have been doing it for so long at one place and you have so many good memories and made a lot of good friends it is even harder. Luckily I am still good friends with a lot of people from there.

I know that the lack of permanent roles is one thing many in the industry struggle with, do you think it will ever change or is just the nature of our industry?

This won't change until the industry takes a good look at how projects are organised and realise that the industry is too far spread to support the model of expanding during full production and then shrinking the team until the next project is ready to go into production and start to have multiple projects in pre-production while the current project is in production. Doing it this way would ensure that once a game has finished production the next one is ready to start full production.

How did you originally get into the industry and did you do anything unique to increase your chances?

My first job came from an application that I didn't think I would hear back from, but then if you're not out there trying you'll never get it. I think the thing that made me stand out was the fact that I had tested table top games for Games Workshop because I was friends with the local store manager at the time so I was always there when early focus testing was done on new games and rule sets, the fact that I was actively submitting issues during Beta test for P.C. games. It is always good to show that you have knowledge, that the job isn't just playing games and that you know what will be expected of you if you are offered the role.

How did you get into your current role?

Networking. One of the things that is really important in the industry is to make sure that people know who you are and get them thinking "this role needs filling, they will be good for it" that gets your foot in the door and then it's a case of reinforcing that impression at the interview. I knew my current Q.A. Manager before I got the role, so when the role came up she knew I was looking for work, told me about the role and was able to give me a recommendation to the head of the company who was doing the hiring.

What advice would you give to people looking to be a Q.A. tester in the industry?

Actually perform testing before you apply for a role whether by participating in Beta tests for games or volunteer for testing mods and be very active with submitting issues. I say this for two reasons:

1. Not everyone enjoys testing over playing as there is a lot more work than most people realize.

2. When you get that interview you have more to back you up than just "I love games" which will make you stand out.

So we both know working in Q.A. can be very repetitive by its nature, do you have any advice for people out there regarding this aspect of your role?

The best way to get through the repetitive aspects of Q.A. is to make personal challenges of those sections. This is where learning about other aspects of production really pays off as you start to become aware of what could break that section and so make the test more varied and interesting.

If hiring would you put more emphasis on education or experience?

For games Q.A. I would say experience (either professional or gained from Beta testing/mod testing) is more beneficial as there isn't a qualification specifically aimed at it.

Do you have any final thoughts for people hoping to become a Q.A. tester in the games industry?

Research everything you can about how games are made as this will give you a better idea of how to test each area of the game

With regards to actually working in the industry, what would you say is the best thing about your role?

Working with people who are all putting everything they have into a game, it creates one of the best work environments I've ever had the pleasure of working in.

What's the worst thing about your role?

Working long hours on very tedious tasks like checking that the menus are working correctly or walking around every inch of a level to make sure the character doesn't fall through the world

So what's an average day for a Q.A. tester like?

It's a cliché, but there isn't really an "average" day as anything can happen. The general structure of any day is the Lead Tester gives you an area of the game to focus on which you test and enter bugs into the database and then when a new build comes in you regress any issues that the development team has fixed.

Do you have any tips for surviving crunch?

Stock up on food and drink that gives you energy as the hardest thing to do is stay awake and keep focused on the task you are doing. Sometimes the best thing you can do when you are struggling with a problem is to walk away and make yourself a drink. It's amazing how often it is that when you come back from making the drink you can work through what was so frustrating just a few minutes before. Also never look at the clock.

So what are the longest hours you've worked during a crunch?

The longest consecutive hours I've worked is 24 hours, the most gruelling though would be me working a night shift and leaving the office at 10 a.m. only to come back in at 3 p.m. the same day to test the new build before it was sent off for submission.

If you could change one thing about the industry what would that be?

The main thing I would change about the industry is how Q.A. is viewed as at the moment a lot of people view Q.A. as "one of those necessary evils that need to be kept at arm's length" rather than an integral part of the process.

Do you think that view is changing? Are Q.A. already becoming thought of as a more than a hurdle?

This is changing slowly. As games are getting bigger and more complex more people are seeing the value of what Q.A. does. At the moment I have found out that the smaller the company the more they value Q.A. as a department.

How do you feel about the challenges women face in the industry?

Women face a lot more challenges than men in the industry largely in part to the fact that it is still very much seen as a boys' club and women are often viewed with the "what are you doing here, you're a girl you don't know anything about games" mentality and that needs to change it the industry is to continue to grow.

Do you think attitudes to women are changing in the industry?

Slowly, I think as more women enter the industry and more and more people are working with more female co-workers they are realizing that it doesn't matter what gender a person is to be able to do the job. As an industry we are working towards a solution to this issue, but we still have a long way to go.

Do you feel women need to work harder to prove themselves in the industry?

With the way a lot of people think about female gamers it takes a lot more for them to prove to the people that they are working with that they are capable of doing the job than it does for a male.

If you could offer one piece of advice to someone starting out in the industry what would that be?

Any chance you have to learn about other disciplines either within your department or another department you should jump at it as not only will it make you better at your role, but people appreciate you taking the time to understand things from their point of view and will then be much more happy with making time to help you with what you need, which makes the whole process better for everyone.

Name:	Nick Scurr	**Currently working for:**	FreeStyleGames ltd
Age:	28	**Current role:**	Senior Q.A. Technician
Sex:	M	**Length of Service:**	3.5 Years (7 years overall)

Nick and I met on a gaming forum. He was happy to share his thoughts and experiences with us.

Why did you want to get into the games industry?

I'd been playing games since a very young age when I was bought an Atari ST as a gift. As I got older and people around me started to decide what they wanted to do after school and university I thought about this hobby that I had been enjoying most of my life and decided I wanted help create the things that I enjoyed the most.
I always wanted to be a tester and had no ambitions to use it as a stepping ladder into Design or some other area. I wanted to help make games as good as they could be.

How long have you worked in the industry?

I've been working in the games industry for 7 years.

Who have you worked for in the industry?

I have worked for Blitz Games Studios and FreeStyleGames.

What do you do in the industry?

I'm a Senior Q.A. Technician for a development studio. Some of the jobs I do here are:
- Leading teams of testers (I'm usually a platform lead if it's a multi-platform project).
- Functionality testing, TRCs/TCRs and design feedback.
- Interviewing new members of staff for the Q.A. department.
- Writing detailed build notes and matrixes for internal and outsourced Q.A. (These are also relayed to Production for milestone checks).
- Help with management of outsourced Q.A., providing tasks and feedback.
- Providing basic training on various Q.A. tools and methods to internal and external studios.

- Working closely with the Dev. Team providing feedback on builds, attending meetings and general help with recreating issues from external Q.A. departments.
- Main point of contact within the company for the bug database we use.
- Setting up new databases.
- Uploading builds, DLC and title updates to the publisher.
- Some community management work (in game message uploads).
- Checking and providing feedback on marketing.

What would you say is the highlight of your career so far?

Working on the DJ Hero series; my first big budget titles. They gave me a lot of experience working with larger teams and were very rewarding for my personal development.

So what would you consider the lowlight of your career so far?

The company I work for went into consultation (administration) last year. This was due to our parent company closing down their music development arm. Being a music game development studio this obviously put us in a bad position. We spent around 90 days in consultation which wasn't nice for anyone. Thankfully this was resolved and the company is still here and doing really well. This situation seems to be ever more common in our industry unfortunately.

How did you originally get into the industry and did you do anything unique to increase your chances?

After I had completed my university course I used a website that collated all the dev. studios in the U.K. and looked through job listings and gathered e-mail addresses. I then emailed as many as I could, regardless of jobs being advertised, with my C.V. proactively looking for work. As I had no experience, I wrote up a report on my favourite game at the time; Metal Gear Solid on the PS One. This contained bugs that I had found in the game along with repro steps. I think the fact that I showed I understood the basics of the job really helped people see past the fact that I had no industry experience. In the end I went to three interviews at Blitz Games Studios, Codemasters and Lionhead and was offered a role at each of these putting me in the lucky position of being able to choose which to go for.

That sounds very similar to what I did to get my first break. Do you think that such methods still work or do people starting out need to adopt more creative methods to get into the industry today?

I think it's increasingly harder to stand out when applying for Q.A. jobs. Recently there seems to have been an increase in applications from those that have been on college/university games courses. These applications usually come with a website containing a portfolio of work. However more often than not, this is detrimental to their application due to spelling mistakes, the quality of the site and the work itself.

If I was starting from the bottom now and trying to get an Interview there are a few extra things I'd try:

I'd take one of the games the company I'm applying to has released and find some bugs in it, hoping not to rub the Q.A. manager up the wrong way obviously! I'd also draw up a test plan (or a partial one) for the same game to try and show my understanding of the process and how I would structure my testing. All that being said 99% of the applications I've seen recently have been standard C.V. and covering letters so maybe the above isn't needed!

How did you get into your current role?

I worked at Blitz Games Studios for 3.5 years. My manager started there shortly after me. We had a meeting one day and he told me he was leaving the company to go to FreeStyleGames to setup a new Q.A. department there. I joined him there a few months later as their new secret project (DJ Hero) took shape to help with this.

What advice would you give to people looking to be a Lead Tester in the industry?

It can be quite hard to get a foot in the door as a tester nowadays. There are a lot of testers out of work who are one step ahead as they have experience. However this can also lead them to sometimes become sloppy with their applications. To make you stand out against those with experience:

- Write a good covering letter to go with your C.V. explaining why you'd like the job and why you feel you'd be the best person for it. You need to say more than 'I love playing video games all day!'

- Keep the C.V. short and to the point. Only include relevant information such as any team based work you have done, working to deadlines etc.
- Attach a game report or gather some bugs that show you can do the job.
- Do some research into the development process if you don't already know it. See how Q.A. fits into that and look into the different types of Q.A. teams that exist.
- Do your research on the companies you're applying to as this will prove very useful should you get an interview.
- The most important thing to do is proof read your application. Bad spelling and grammar usually result in an instant 'no' decision. Q.A. requires great attention to detail so don't fall at the first hurdle!

If hiring would you put more emphasis on education or experience?

Q.A. does not really have any 'course' associated with it (yet), so I mostly look for those that try to stand out and show genuine enthusiasm for the job, experienced or not. After all everyone has to start somewhere so I always make sure that whenever we have a position we get a good mix of those with and without experience.

So what qualities do you think a good tester needs?

- Attention to detail. It's very easy to let an issue slip past when you've been playing the same game for months on end.
- Be very descriptive when writing bug reports. Imagine that someone has not seen the game before and will be using your steps to recreate the issue; the dev. team don't always play the game.
- Be diplomatic. Bugs should not be written in a confrontational way. Likewise if a member of the dev. team leaves an unhelpful comment you must deal with it in a professional manner.
- Work well as part of a team. Communicate! You can cover the game a whole lot easier if you're working as one. Duplicating bug reports wastes time.
- Be proactive. Read the design document for the project and look at the upcoming features so that you can plan ahead.
- Being able to ask for help. There's a lot to learn and each studio has its own practices. Don't be afraid to get someone to show you any programs/software/features you don't quite understand. It will help to make you into a better tester.

Do you have any final thoughts for people hoping to become a Lead Tester in the games industry?

Don't be disheartened by any rejection letters you get, ask for feedback if possible and adapt. Keep applying to as many studios/publishers as you can. Every reply, interview, rejection letter is experience to build upon. Take part in Beta tests to get a feel of what it's like to play unpolished games. Be prepared to move/travel for your dream job. Dev. studios tend to be bunched up in certain areas so you might have to make a few sacrifices to get in.

With regards to actually working in the industry, what would you say is the best thing about your role?

The best thing about my role is the people I work with. Everyone is a likeminded bunch and we all love the work we do. I love playing games and I get to work and chat with people that do the same. I also get paid to do what I love, a rare thing indeed so I'm told!

What's the worst thing about your role?

The uncertainty of the industry is a worry. I have a family and sometimes it can feel like you can only see as far ahead as the end of the current project which isn't nice when trying to plan for the future.

So what's an average day for a Lead Tester like?

I'm usually the first in so will check that the builds are all there ready for the day's testing.
I'll check my E-mails for any project information or test requests from the development team. We will then have a Q.A. team meeting and discuss the previous day's work, any major issues and then sort out the work for the day with tasks assigned to each team member.
The remainder is then filled with meetings, testing and checking bug fixes!

Do you have any tips for surviving crunch?

As a junior it can be hard to say no to all the overtime during a busy period. Don't forget in most instances you're volunteering your own time and not being paid. Don't be afraid to say no if you have plans. It's really important to maintain a healthy work/life balance.

So what are the longest hours you've worked during a crunch?

I've done a few 15/16 hour shifts. I was a lot younger at the time and it was made easier due to the team being a good group. However I would not allow myself to work these kinds of hours now that I'm a bit wiser and older; I'd rather be at home with my family.

In that case would you consider the games industry or at least crunch as a young man's game?

I think crunch is a young man's game in that they are sometimes knowingly exploited. When you first start you're so grateful for the job and want to use every available opportunity to impress your lead/boss. However, I don't think I've ever seen someone be promoted/let go based on the overtime they have worked, it just seems to make the higher ups look good!

If you could change one thing about the industry what would that be?

I'd like the production/management teams to take better control of the projects. This includes managing the timescales of the project correctly so that crunch is not necessary. The schedule should allow for extra time during normal hours as a backup. A lot of the time it seems as though the overtime is factored in as regular man hours to be used on the project! Overtime should be an exception, not the rule.

Do you think attitudes to crunch are changing or is it largely staying the same? Is it perhaps company dependant?

I think the dev. teams want them to change. No-one wants to be doing it. Maybe it's indirectly marketing led. They pick a date when your game is going to release and you need to hit that date. I don't believe they take into account how long it will take to actually make the game when they set that date though!

It's definitely gotten better each year in my experience.

How do you feel about the challenges women face in the industry?

I personally don't think it's harder for women to get a role in this industry, though I can't really speak for outside of Q.A. We certainly have far fewer women applying than men for roles in my department. There just doesn't seem to be as much interest. Maybe this is because women that would like to join see it as male dominated and as such don't apply.

Do you think attitudes to women are changing in the industry?

I can't say I have ever encountered an 'attitude' towards women in the industry (maybe I've just been lucky). However, I know outside of my company that there are lecturers, groups and talks that go on to promote women in games and these are a lot more prominent than when I started 7 years ago which can only be a positive thing.

Do you feel women need to work harder to prove themselves in the industry?

I'd hope that the only pressure they feel is to do the job to the best of their ability and not worry about being judged based on their sex. Where I work I don't think there is a difference. Everyone works hard and isn't judged one way or the other. I wouldn't want to work somewhere where this wasn't the case!

Nick it's been a pleasure getting to know you for this interview, thanks for your time.

Name:	Nelson de Gouveia	**Currently working for:**	IdeaWorks3D
Age:	31	**Current role:**	Lead Tester
Sex:	Male	**Length of Service:**	8 years

Another old colleague turned friend, Nelson has spent many years in Q.A. and has a wealth of experience to share.

Why did you want to get into the games industry?

Never expected to, I was one of the lucky "few" whose random C.V. dropped on a recruiter's lap and changed my life forever. As I've been a videogames player all my life, that wasn't exactly a bad day.

How long have you worked in the industry?

8 years now. I've moved around from company to company and briefly worked as a Producer, which was an absolute joy.

Who have you worked for in the industry?

SEGA was the first one, then smaller publishing and development houses around the country, once did a stint in Germany. That was fun.

What do you do in the industry?

I've been mainly doing Quality Assurance, finding issues within videogame projects and reporting them to the development teams to fix. But my skills range towards production, project management, copywriting, marketing, video and graphics editing. I even wrote dialogue scripts for a few smaller games.

Q.A. is still very much seen as a route into the industry. Do you think that's still the case or has it become much more of a career path in its own right?

It's definitely more of a career path now as I've seen individuals go on to run their own departments in other studios. In addition, it's not the only route anymore, just the only route for inexperienced individuals (I can be honest about it, I had no project or team management experience prior to going into Q.A.).

What would you say is the highlight of your career so far?

Definitely getting a positive review for the dialogue in a game I adored writing for.

So what would you consider the lowlight of your career so far?

Getting a bad review for the game itself.

Do you think reviews are a fair system as after all it is just one person's opinion?

You and the team either made a good game or a bad game. Reviews are there to tell the users, which is which, so my own opinion is to make a good game and you get good reviews.

How did you originally get into the industry and did you do anything unique to increase your chances?

I was unemployed for a few weeks after a few years working as a P.R. assistant and a recruiter called asking if I wanted a 3 month testing stint at SEGA. My availability definitely was one factor, but dedication to the craft and just being passionate about completing a project to budget and deadline.

What advice would you give to people looking to be a lead tester in the industry?

Besides talking to the recruitment agencies? It doesn't hurt to send out your C.V. to all the companies you can find that you're able to commute to. However, as these are all creative companies, some sort of expression might make you stand out. Personalities are a boon in this business.

If hiring would you put more emphasis on education or experience?

Most of the time I wouldn't consider either really, but upon recommendation. It's a sad fact, but companies involved in nepotism eventually do well as they tend to work closer and are far more productive. Having said that, experience.

Do you have any final thoughts for people hoping to become a lead tester in the games industry?

When you're younger, it's a dream job, but keep in mind that it's still a business and you're not there for fun. Someone has placed an investment in you and they require that you deliver to their expectations. The rewards themselves far outweigh your bragging rights to your mates down the pub.

With regards to actually working in the industry, what would you say is the best thing about your role?

The people and the challenges, both are constant, fresh and always interesting.

What's the worst thing about your role?

The disappointment of not finding every problem.

So what's an average day for a lead tester like?

Get in on time, sitting down with a device (in my case currently, a mobile device), check for the latest version, go through morning team meetings, complete any tasks needed and report to the Producer

Do you have any tips for surviving crunch?

Avoid smoking and drinking. Enjoy your coffee and tea, but too much caffeine will make you twitch, try to relax whenever you can as your body needs the small bits of downtime required.

So what are the longest hours you've worked during a crunch?

22 hours.

If you could change one thing about the industry what would that be?

The fragmented natures of devices, such a wide variety that people can enjoy, but for the industry it's a nightmare to convert the same game to many different types of hardware. Having said that, building the same game between higher- and lower-spec machines (i.e. from console to handheld) brings up many design challenges that definitely improve and change the industry as we know it.

How do you feel about the challenges women face in the industry?

It's a shame that there are any as there's no specific difference between men and women other than biology.

Do you think attitudes to women are changing in the industry?

It's constantly evolving, but it has been parallel to universal work practices for other industries. In the old days they were confined to serving tea and cakes for the IBM programmers, now they're polishing off their stock portfolios and making other fools look foolish.

Do you feel women need to work harder to prove themselves in the industry?

Not anymore, but if they still have to beside their workmates, they shouldn't be working for a company that employs such people in the first place.

If you could offer one piece of advice to someone starting out in the industry what would that be?

It's a job, work hard.

Do you think too many people come into the industry expecting a laugh, to mess about or to bask in the glory of creating without any of the actual backbreaking work we do? It's certainly one of the reasons I wrote this book to try to give people a realistic expectation of our working world.

I've seen people take their role less than serious; heck, I myself admit my workmates have suffered my lethargy too often. But it's a minor amount and, despite the laughter and play, we're all in it to make good games, to be part of an experience, to feel good about what we grew up with and we're contributing towards and so most of us still put the hours in and work hard.

Name:	Marc Robinson	***Currently working for:***	Beeline, Capcom
Age:	30	***Current role:***	Q.A.Tester
Sex:	M	***Length of Service:***	2 months

Marc has all the fine qualities of a tester, hard working and experienced he was the perfect choice for an interview.

Why did you want to get into the games industry?

I've very much grown up as one of the computer/console generation kids. Started off with a Dragon 32 all those years ago and always tried to get my hands on any new console that came along. Even got myself a Vectrex (which I imagine most people reading this will have to Google). The Dragon was great simply because it allowed you to program and rewrite games with considerable ease. Think I was about 7 or 8 when I wrote my first game, a text RPG based on the house I was living in at the time. As I moved on to consoles I stopped playing around with programming and seemed to gain a strange enjoyment by making games do things they weren't supposed to do. Strangely though, I never actually considered going in to the games industry as an actual career. After flirting with genetics in secondary school I ended up choosing music and followed it through to university in London. During my third year, a job in the games industry turned up and I though "Why not?"

How long have you worked in the industry?

I've been a paid member of the industry for around five years, though I started out Beta testing games several years before that.

Do you feel that Beta testing helped you to secure your first job in the industry?

Without a doubt, yes. I went to the interview knowing I could do the job and they knew it too. Confidence in your abilities is very important.

Who have you worked for in the industry?

My longest stint would be with Sega Europe, but I've also worked at Sports Interactive, Microsoft, TT Games and now Beeline, Capcom.

What do you do in the industry?

I started out as a Q.A. tester and worked my way up to be in charge of a team of 20 testers after a few years, but I found that the higher you got in the industry, the less time you actually spent hands-on with the games. When I left that job I made the decision to go back to being a tester again, even though the money isn't great, simply because I love being up to my elbows in the games and doing everything I can to make them do things they're not meant to be doing.

What would you say is the highlight of your career so far?

My first job with Sports Interactive and my current job at Beeline have been the most enjoyable times I've spent in the industry. From a Q.A. perspective you just can't beat working alongside the development team. Your input and performance becomes so much more important and the challenges it presents are fantastic. The one thing I'm most proud of, this is going to make me sound like a major Q.A. geek, isn't actually something I've done while working, but at home with a retail game. Nintendo are incredibly thorough with their own IPs and the chances of a major issue making it through to release are tiny, but I found a way of locking up one of their biggest games which forced you to restart. Told you it was geeky...

So what would you consider the lowlight of your career so far?

Not really a lowlight, but my time running my own test team is the least enjoyment I've had in the industry. The challenges it presented were engaging, but the work itself just wasn't what I wanted to be doing. Instead of working directly with the games themselves, I'd spend every day in the bugs' database looking over other people's work, writing reports and other such tasks which kept me away from actually testing the game.

So would you say it's better to do what you love over career progression?

It depends what you want from life, really. From a personal point of view, Q.A. gives just enough financial reward to live comfortably and I enjoy going to work every day. I'd prefer that over a well paid job where you have to fight just to get yourself to work each morning.

How did you originally get into the industry and did you do anything unique to increase your chances?

While not unique, I think my entrance in to the games industry is reasonably rare. I'd spent a lot of time playing Championship Manager and then Football Manager when the development team split from their publisher and went their own way, I eventually found their online forums. After a few months on there, reporting bugs in the game, providing and discussing suggestions and game feedback, I was invited to be part of their Beta test team. After a few years of doing this, with my university course about to finish, I was invited down for an interview to work in-house with the development team. I got the job (and worked there instead of attending the final year of University course) and it all went from there. I left after 6 months and finished off my final year in far too short a time period, but by then I'd decided to join the games industry as a career.

How did you get into your current role?

This is going to sound very straightforward, but I left my last job once my contract had expired, applied for this one and got it.

What advice would you give to people looking to be a tester in the industry?

You must have enthusiasm. A lot of companies are happy to hire testers with no previous experience as long as they show enthusiasm and an eye for detail. There are times when what you are asked to do can be very boring (think of your favourite game, now imagine having to play one level of that game over and over again, every day for a week, now imagine doing it on a game you might not like. You need to make sure your performance doesn't drop in such situations and a true enthusiasm for what you're doing is one of the best ways to maintain it.

If hiring would you put more emphasis on education or experience?

In testing, experience is far more important than education. In other roles, education becomes more important. There are things in testing you can't learn about without actually doing them. You start to get a feel of when a game is close to breaking, your past experience will also hint at what you could do to push the game over the edge and actually break it.

I know that when we started out there were no courses in Q.A. These have started appearing recently. How do you feel about studying games Q.A.?

I've done a little bit of research into Q.A. courses and they do seem beneficial to people hoping to move into Q.A. They should help you get your first role. However, when it comes down to hiring, I'd still value experience over someone with a Q.A. course to their name. However, if someone had both they should be in a very good position.

Do you have any final thoughts for people hoping to become a tester in the games industry?

It's not an easy job. It's not just sitting there playing games for money. If you approach it thinking otherwise, you will find yourself bored and will not last long in the job.

With regards to actually working in the industry, what would you say is the best thing about your role?

I'm probably not the best person to answer this because as I mentioned earlier I gain enjoyment from simply breaking games, but for a lot of people wanting to work in other roles in the industry, testing is often a great way to get in and network. However, if you use it as just a way to get in, the chances are you'll struggle. The industry is a surprisingly small world, everyone knows someone who knows everyone else. If your performance isn't up to scratch, someone at a company you apply for later on will know about it.

Q.A. has historically been seen as a route into the industry. Earlier in the book we discuss a career in just Q.A. Do you have any thoughts on remaining in Q.A. as a career path in itself?

A career in just Q.A. won't be easy as you really have to love what you're doing to make something of it. If you're like me, want to remain as hands-on with the projects as possible, then it'll be a lot harder making ends meet than someone who would like to progress to other roles.

What's the worst thing about your role?

Job security and wages as a tester aren't the best. Most places offer short term contracts only, the longer contracts tend to have a catch (for example, zero hour contracts are long term, but at any point you could be told there isn't the work available for you and you then go back to being without a job while still under contract). There are a few places that offer permanent contracts, but with everyone else in the industry also after those roles it can be very difficult to get them. Some places pay better than others, but don't expect to go splashing the cash as a tester, especially if you're inexperienced.

So what's an average day for a tester like?

You'll usually have a task waiting for you when you arrive in the mornings. It could be playing through the game from start to finish, concentrating on one level over and over again, reading through all the text in the game etc. The tasks are often varied and rotated so you'll find yourself doing everything to every part of the game at some point or other, but two days in a row are very unlikely to be the same.

Do you have any tips for surviving crunch?

Bring lots of Tangfastics. The sugar helps a lot when you feel yourself starting to flag a little. Crunch periods often include some crazy work hours and you really need to enjoy what you do to keep up with it.

So what are the longest hours you've worked during a crunch?

12 hour crunch shifts are the norm, but the craziest period would have been three 24 hour shifts in a row with 12 hours off in between. I may be a bit strange here, but I found it incredibly fun to do that.

If you could change one thing about the industry what would that be?

The recognition of how important the Q.A. process actually is. Those that prove they are good at their jobs shouldn't have to move off to a different role in order to improve their income, they should be offered a higher wage to continue doing what they're doing.

Do you think attitudes to Q.A. are changing in the industry? Is it becoming more valued as we mature as an industry?

In some companies Q.A. is starting to get the recognition it deserves. It's an incredibly important part of games development and certain figures in the industry are really fighting for it, especially those who have risen to their current roles by working their way through Q.A.

How do you feel about the challenges women face in the industry?

Gaming is no longer just a boy's toy, everyone plays games these days. In testing I have worked with a lot of women and there's no discrimination that I can see. Your promotion and job prospects don't hinge on what sex you are, but on what you can offer the company as an employee.

Do you think attitudes to women are changing in the industry?

In Q.A. I've never seen anything that suggests attitudes are altered depending on the sex of the employee. Everyone pretty much gets along as they would if they were friends outside of work.

Do you feel women need to work harder to prove themselves in the industry?

Everyone needs to work hard in Q.A. and at the end of the day that's what's important. If you do your job well, it doesn't matter who you are.

If you could offer one piece of advice to someone starting out in the industry what would that be?

Make sure this is something you want to do as it can be tough and unreliable. Remember, it's not just playing games for money.

Name:	Leo Tan	**Currently working for:**	Capcom
Age:	35	**Current role:**	Senior P.R. Manager (U.K.)
Sex:	Male	**Length of Service:**	Four years

I met Leo at an industry event through a friend. He was happy to chat about his experiences in the industry.

Why did you want to get into the games industry?

Simply put, I love games. I'm old enough to have been there from the beginning and I've watched gaming develop into what it is today. I love them, I spend more time gaming than anything other than sleeping and working and even then it's probably a close call.

How long have you worked in the industry?

Around seven years.

Who have you worked for in the industry?

I started at Barrington Harvey Public Relations. In my two and a half years there I worked on anything from obscure P.C. simulators to Guild Wars and Guitar Hero. When Activision bought RedOctane, I followed Guitar Hero and went to work at Activision for a measly 11 months before I received my true calling in life; helping Capcom re-launch Street Fighter. I think that went quite well.

What do you do in the industry?

I'm a publicist, which means it's my job to make sure that the games I work on are as visible as possible. If you read about one of my games and it's not an advert, I was almost definitely involved in that coverage in some way.

What would you say is the highlight of your career so far?

Single-handedly reviving fighting games in the U.K. I mean, sure, I didn't make Street Fighter IV and sure the game had that effect in every other country in the world. However, my absence in those countries implies that I probably didn't make that much difference, but taking credit for other people's work is something every publicist has to do. I'm just taking the process to another level.

So what would you consider the lowlight of your career so far?

The worst part about my job is the sheer volume of hatred that I have to process every day. It's not specific to me, everyone I know in the games industry that has any kind of public profile has to deal with it. We all receive hate mail and the odd death threat any time. Something happens that someone doesn't like and you'll always do something that someone doesn't like. Gamers are extremely passionate about what they do, which is brilliant, but sadly they're also capable of extremely rude and callous behaviour that has reduced plenty of people to tears, usually over something quite trivial. You do learn to ignore it, but I do wish I hadn't learned how to be so capable of switching off. When you learn how to do that you lose something important.

How did you originally get into the industry and did you do anything unique to increase your chances?

I was an average hairdresser with enough free time to spend probably 20-30 hours a week on the old Edge forum. At the time it was one of the only gaming forums in existence (that I knew of anyway) and so was full of industry people. Lots of my friends were games journalists and they'd always moan about how terrible P.R.s were. One of them urged me to get into P.R. so I sent Simon Byron (then director of Barrington Harvey PR) a begging letter and after a bit of polite badgering he gave me a job.

Luck and networking has been mentioned a fair bit by the other interviewees. Do you think you would have got into the industry if you hadn't networked on the Edge forums?

I sincerely doubt it. I was very lucky to have met the people I did, but I was also lucky in that there were very few places to go in those days. Forums were quite a new thing and so it wasn't hard to be in the right place at the right time. If I was enthusing about my top 10 Dreamcast games today, it's unlikely anyone would even hear me, such is the noise level right now. I would still say networking is of the utmost importance and if you're in the U.K. then being in London probably helps, but other than that I don't know how anyone would go about it. The scene is quite established now, with so much talent to choose from for any particular role that you'd need to be much more excellent than we ever were back in the day just to be heard. I've seen so many passionate, talented interns working super hard that still struggle to land a proper job. It's tough.

How did you get into your current role?

I think the two biggest factors in getting my first job were knowing lots of journalists already and having a writing style that Simon Byron liked. It was also just quite lucky that I wanted a job at the same time as he had a vacancy. Luck has been a huge factor in most of my career so far.

What advice would you give to people looking to be a P.R. manager in the industry?

Have something more to offer than a solid passion for games. Passion for games is important, but it's not distinctive. 99 of every 100 applicants for any games industry position, regardless of the discipline, will have that passion. I would say that you don't even need the contacts, just have an understanding of the discipline, a strong work ethic and patience. Try to get a job at one of the larger P.R. agencies and learn the trade. Develop the skills, then come to us and you'll maximize your chances of success. Even then, always keep in mind that luck is probably still the biggest factor (if luck can be considered a factor at all).

Although you don't have crunch as such, is there much overtime or anti-social hours in your role?

YES. There is a crazy amount of travelling and working weekends. Public events will almost always happen outside of normal working hours and there's usually another country to visit every other month. Any job that works to deadlines results in working overtime to meet those deadlines. That's why you need endurance and a positive outlook.

If hiring would you put more emphasis on education or experience?

Experience every time. That said, our two most recent P.R. hires both have P.R. degrees, but they were hired based on their year's internship in the games industry rather than the knowledge the degree represents.

Do you have any final thoughts for people hoping to become a P.R. manager in the games industry?

I cannot stress this enough, write well. I will not consider interviewing somebody whose cover letter or C.V. isn't well written. Don't even consider sending either in with a typo. A typo will have your application thrown in the bin without hesitation, it shows a lack of attention to detail in what should be one of the most important tasks you'll perform in life. What does that say about your work if a task is less important? If you can't write well, you should look for a different discipline.

So is your role primarily writing or do you need a keen eye for screenshots and other art work?

If you know games then you'll know what makes a good screenshot. Choosing assets is easy, not the least because you'll often be given them by someone who knows the game inside out anyway. What I'd be looking for in a new team member is writing ability, endurance, persistence and a positive attitude. But definitely writing ability, since most of your communication will be textual and great hair. You need to have great hair.

With regards to actually working in the industry, what would you say is the best thing about your role?

Seeing games early. It feels like you're in a secret club and everyone else in that club loves the things that you love and everyone has a special key to a vault that contains all of those things. It's juvenile, but so am I.

What's the worst thing about your role?

The internet hate, but as I've said, I'm pretty thick-skinned these days.

If you could reply to the critics on the internet honestly, what would you like to tell them?

I talk to critics on a daily basis and I'm always honest. I don't have anything left unsaid. I think that's important. I've seen some publicists let things build up inside and then have spectacular meltdowns. Don't be one of those people. Have honest, open, friendly relationships and everyone wins. P.R. can feel like war on a daily basis or it can be friends hanging out, talking about the things we love the most. We get to choose which of those it is and I'll always choose the latter when I can.

So what's an average day for a P.R. manager like?

Probably 50 per cent of any day is simply reacting to questions from the press about the games you have coming out in the next 12 months, regardless of what you've already told them. Usually you don't have the information they want or you'd already have made it public and they wouldn't need to call you, but we still go through the motions. The rest of my day is spent planning what I'm going to do with my games over the next six months, meeting with agencies to brainstorm ideas, reading as much media as my time allows and sometimes, just sometimes, I get to play a game I'm working on.

If you could change one thing about the industry what would that be?

I'd change the games media's fascination with both outrageous hit-grabbing headlines and the need to pigeonhole every single game into a confined set of market-appropriate features. Most games journalists I know got into the game because they love gaming and writing and after a few years they're hell bent on punishing a game because it's not exactly how they'd design it, which I think is a shame. As to the headlines, I'm not sure how to address that beyond changing the business model to revolve around something other than ad serves. At least it's a predictable system, if nothing else. That makes life easier for people like me.

To some extent do you feel that games reviewers have too much power?

Saying games reviewers have 'power' implies there's some kind of real battle going on and that games' reviewers need to be defeated. While I won't say that the romantic notion you've presented doesn't appeal to the gamer in me, I will say that the correlation between reviews and sales has been much argued over in many industries and that I have no conclusive proof or opinion. I'm sure you could equally argue that publicists have "too much power", whatever that is. Reviewers will review games, we will supply the games to be reviewed. That's all that's going on. My job is to enable the review, their job is to provide the review. I feel that we cannot really exist without one another.

How do you feel about the challenges women face in the industry?

I have no idea what challenges women face in our industry. Perhaps in development it's different, but in publishing I've not seen any women particularly struggling to make a name for themselves. But I'm in no position to comment.

Do you think attitudes to women are changing in the industry?

Again, I'm not equipped to answer this question. I haven't worked anywhere that has made things difficult for a woman.

If you could offer one piece of advice to someone starting out in the industry what would that be?

Become amazing at what you do. Care about your skill-set more than the games and don't be afraid to make choices that take you away from the games that you love. The more brilliant you are at what you do, the more easily you'll be able to work wherever you want and the chances are that your dream job today will not necessarily be your dream job tomorrow. Flexibility is the key.

Name:	Tom Champion	***Currently working for:***	Eurogamer
Age:	31	***Current role:***	Community Manager
Sex:	Male	***Length of Service:***	2.5 Years

I've known Tom for many years as an industry recruiter; since he joined Eurogamer I've watched him organize the U.K.'s largest gaming event. An amazingly talented guy, it was great to find out how he manages such an event year on year.

Why did you want to get into the games industry?

I've only ever wanted to work in games really. To go back a bit, when I was a kid I just loved games and wanted to be in it, but had no aptitude for math, or science or art, so a lot of those traditional roles in game development were closed off to me because I was never going to be able to do A-levels in math or science, the stuff that will take you onto doing programming, art or design or anything like that. So I was a little bit stuck, didn't really know what to do. I graduated in 2002 with a business degree which was never going to help me get into games in any way at all and I'd kind of given up the dream of working in games. I did one stupid thing when I was just graduated. I went for an interview at Codemasters for a Q.A. job, turned up in a suit with no idea. I hadn't really thought about how I was going to relocate to Leamington Spa on six pound an hour, was generally clueless and no surprise I didn't get it. Didn't do very well at the testing test. I was appalling, I think I found like one bug or something. It was woeful. So then I sort of gave up and moved to London in 2004 without a job. I was looking around and I saw an advert on a website called Games Recruit. A company, a recruitment company, was looking for recruitment agents to work as an agent recruiting people into games developers and publishers. It wasn't really kind of a suitable job for me in any way as I'm not a recruitment guy, I'm not a sales' guy. No interest in that, but the one thing was that it was involved in the games industry and I thought it might open up doors later on. So that's what I did. I applied for this job as a game's recruiter, got it, then spent about four or five years doing recruitment in games, which was really tough for me because, as I say, it wasn't a job I ideally was suited to.

Kind of a bit perverse really. You were helping people do exactly what you wanted to but weren't able to do yourself

Yeah, exactly! It was completely weird, but it was great. I got to talk to a lot of people who made games, some great games, as well as talk to a lot of high level people. Being involved in recruitment, you get an idea of how the industry works, how each of the departments work and it was good from that perspective. I learnt a lot and obviously met a lot of people as well, including the Eurogamer guys, which is why I eventually ended up being here when my last recruitment job finished and I was at a loose end. Luckily I just happened to be down here in Brighton and they needed someone for the 2009 Expo.

So bizarrely, without meaning to, you actually spent a few years networking and I suppose that must have stood you in good stead here because you have contacts when it comes to chatting about the Expo, getting people involved with their games. You're a bit of a name yourself.

Yeah, in a way, I suppose so. It has been really good because you get to hear from people, from back in the day that I knew (when I worked in recruiting) that I'm now in contact with through the Expo and other stuff, so yeah, it's good. I mean, the U.K. industry is not that big, so in some ways it is kind of easy to get to know the key people at different companies and stuff.

The phrase is incestuous. Throughout the industry there's always someone you've worked with previously or who knows someone you worked with as you know.

Unless people bugger off to Canada, otherwise they tend to stick around and do the tour of all the various studios and publishers, a bit like you have really.

So what's a day like for a Community Manager? And I guess what's a day like around Expo time for an Expo guy?

Very different. So, my view of community management is that you act as a bridge between the people consuming whatever it is your guys are creating. So if I was working on a game, say I was working on the new F1 game, I'd be the guy who was the voice between the people playing that game and the guys who were making it. But in this case the game happens to be a website, I'm the guy feeding back what our users, what our readers, are thinking and saying and I'm feeding that back to the company. It's just like making sure you're aware of what they want and trying to make them happy. There's also feedback from Eurogamer to the readers as well, about what's going on and all that sort of thing. So it's just really a bridge thing and it's about creating a nice, good, atmosphere. I mean, it's not necessarily about driving more traffic to the website as such, although I think driving traffic and also selling games, if I was working on a game, can be a by-product of good community management, but I think the idea is that you create a better, more vibrant, interesting atmosphere for your existing users primarily. That's kind of what I try to do as Eurogamer's Community Manager.

As regards to the Expo, obviously that's going to be different because not only am I doing community stuff for that, but I'm also doing logistical stuff. So I'm figuring out how many consoles we're going to need, what format, whether the consoles need to be debug or retail, what size TVs we're going to be getting, how tournaments are going to work, how many control pads each game needs, just kind of random networking, I've got a lot of online connectivity to sort.

So who would supply the controllers?

Sony, Nintendo and Microsoft each have like an events company that they use. Microsoft use a company called NJ Live and I think Sony use Amplify and Denim, I think they're called, those guys basically manage events for Sony and Microsoft so those are the guys who tend to supply all the stuff, those are the guys who bring the Xboxes and the Playstations, tend to set them up and stuff. However, we've got to inform them about what we need and all that sort of thing, so that's kind of how that works. There is some stuff that we are completely responsible for so we do the branding. We need to liaise with publishers about branding for their games at the show because we have those big units with images so we have to make sure that we get the artwork from them which we then forward to our guys for signage and that sort of thing. We are also responsible for networking anything that needs internet so we need to liaise with the guys who provide the internet at Earls Court and make sure that all those games are supplied. We also do the networking ourselves so I have to spend loads of time buying network switches and cables. I think I ordered like 400 network cables in the end, 200 USB leads for Playstation controllers and that sort of thing.

Then there's talks, health and safety, it's a phenomenal amount.

Yeah there's a lot of stuff. I mean the good thing is we got partners in key areas, so we have an events company that works with us, who helps us out with a lot of the logistical organisation of actually getting trucks on site and what time that's going to take place, all that sort of thing. There's break down and build and all that sort of stuff, electric lighting, carpets etc...

All the work that goes into it and that's only pre-event!

Yeah it's insane and then actually on the day I'm kind of making sure that everything is just running smoothly, ensuring consoles are on and working, actually functioning because a lot of the time they end up falling over and you have to reset them because its pre-release code I guess. Then it's just being on hand to make sure that the show runs smoothly and fire-fighting problems as they happen.

So you were there working on the Expo in its early days, before it got to Earls Court. What's it like seeing something that starts off as a relatively small, maybe a couple of thousand person event, almost exploding into what it is now?

It's pretty amazing and this year (2011) was a big jump from previous years as you say. In 2009 it still felt like a big event because we did two events in the same week, one in Leeds...

This was when there was almost a split Expo.

Yeah, we did two days in Leeds and then we travelled down and did two days in London. That was a complete nightmare and I don't think we'd ever be able to do that again. We want to do an event outside London, but not in the same week sort of thing. It's been great really, it's grown from a few thousand in 2009 up to... we did 35 thousand visitors in this year and next year I don't know, we will do 40 or 45 thousand. It's been brilliant to see it grow so fast.

Do you feel that you've fulfilled your original hopes and goals of working in the games industry?

My job's brilliant, I absolutely love it. I've really achieved what I wanted to, given that, as I said earlier, there was really no chance of me getting into a mainstream development job as a programmer, artist or designer. So really anything working in games, other than that area would have been a big success for me. Thankfully I've done it and the company here is great and the stuff we're working on is amazing. I couldn't be happier really.

So what would you consider the lowlight and highlight of your career so far?

Lowlight, I think there was a point when I left my first recruitment job because the company had gone downhill, I'd joined another agency and I just found it really tough. I spent 6 months there and I just wasn't getting on with it at all. I'd probably made one placement in the six months that I was at this company, I was feeling really despondent and I wasn't really sure what to do. I left the job, not because I had another job to go to, but because I couldn't stand it anymore and I'd reached the point where I was like "I don't think I'm going to carry on in games any more, I think I'm going to go back to Wales, where my family live, just sit it out and go and get a proper job".

Down the mine?

Yeah exactly, that was the real low point. I'm lucky things didn't work out that way, I took another chance and it worked out. Highlight? Got to be this year's Expo, it was an absolutely brilliant, fantastic, amazing event. I loved every minute, can't wait for next year's to be honest.

For years you worked in recruitment. Do you have any advice for anyone starting out on their career and trying to get that first break into the industry, what can they do to improve their chances?

Yeah, it depends what kind of level you're at. You've got to think, there's so much information around these days and there perhaps wasn't much when I was starting out. I was really naïve, I thought that all you needed was a passion to get into games and you could land a programming job just like that and become a lead programmer. It's not how it works. There's no real shortcuts to that sort of job and if you're going to be a really good programmer you got to go down that traditional route of doing math's 'A' level, a math's degree, just get your fundamentals right. If you're going to be an artist, you've got to learn to draw, do a traditional art degree, all that sort of thing. There's so much information out there now and don't get sucked in by doing stupid pointless degrees with a name like Computer Game Design or something because that probably won't help you. There are no real shortcuts to that sort of job.

However, the flip side is there are loads of different opportunities around now like Community Management is really only a thing that has sprung up in the last few years, I think. People are still trying to define that role and find out what it means. So really there are kind of endless possibilities with it. So yeah, to maximise your chances I would just do your research. Find out what you want to do from an early age and if you don't think you can do programming or design or something, then figure out something else you can do. Are you any good at sales? Could you do marketing, production, maybe do a project manager course. If you're really organised you can get a project manager or producer role at some point. The other thing is, which is what I did, I was really lucky, but also I took opportunities when they arose and they may not have been ideal. Like I never wanted to be a recruitment agent, but if I hadn't ever taken that chance and done that job for a few years there's no way I'd be doing what I'm doing now. So take a chance, even if it looks like something that might not be completely suitable for you. If it's in an area related to games, then just take the chance because it can lead to something else. You might spend a few years doing something you don't really want to do, but ultimately it can lead to doing something that you really love.

In those sorts of situations you can learn, you can network, you can start positioning yourself as a much more suitable candidate for that dream job.

It's all about who you know. Just get to know people and talk to people, people are much more likely to hire people if they know them than if you're just another C.V. on a big pile of C.V.s. Don't pester people, but go to events and just chat. There's loads of game companies, there's loads of publishes that do little events that are just about sampling games, put on a night in a pub somewhere and just invite loads of people. I'm really amazed because we advertise them sometimes on our forum and I'm really surprised that more people don't go along to little events like that because there will be P.R. and marketing people there that you can talk to. Be informed basically, do your research, talk to people.

So if I'm a wet behind the ears graduate and I really wanted to make that first step is it worth me contacting the industry recruitment agents? As a candidate myself I always find it a case of once you had some experience, one or two jobs, they were much more interested in dealing with you than when you had no experience.

It's definitely worth talking to agents. Good agents will actually take the time to talk to you. They may not be able to offer you any sort of jobs to apply for, but they will be able to give you advice if they're good agents. I certainly didn't do it every time, but I tried as much as possible when people like that phoned up, I tried to give them the best advice I could. They will spend about ten-fifteen minutes talking to you. They may not be able to place you, you've got to look at it from the agent's point of view, a company, a publisher or developer is not going to want to pay an agent several thousand pounds to hire a graduate when they could just go to a university and hire them directly. The agent probably won't be able to help you actually get a job, it would be quite rare if they could, but they will at least be able to give you some advice, so it is worth talking to them.

So do you have any final thoughts for people out there who want to be a Community Manager or an Expo organiser? What they might do to help get to that lofty position?

Obviously the Expo role is kind of rare I guess because there's not too many exhibitions, conventions happening, there's a few so it's difficult to go out and want to achieve that job because there aren't many opportunities around. Community wise, I think it's about retaining that passion for gaming because you need to be able to talk to people about games on their level, be able to feedback to them and be able to understand what they're on about. You'd be surprised a lot of people who work in games I find are quite jaded about playing games and they kind of lose that aspect.

I must admit a lot of people I've worked with in games are old gamers. They used to be hardcore gamers and now they have a wife and kids, gaming has slipped off their radar a bit. Since I was in Q.A. I was always one of the most passionate gamers, which is quite shocking. If these people don't engage with their customer, how can they provide products that these guys want?

Yeah it's weird, but that's kind of what happens you get older, get families and stuff there's less time. I've got less time than I once had, but at the same time you've got to actually sit down and make sure you're playing these games, play the latest games. Organise tournaments and stuff. If you eventually want to be a Community Manager make sure you're the guy organising little tournaments and competitions, get yourself on Twitter and Facebook, create groups and stuff. Be the guy who is organising all that stuff and that will really help if you going for community management jobs specifically. The other thing about community management is you have to be able to write as well, so make sure you have a blog and are writing articles. Do write-ups of the tournaments that you do, anything like that, anything that's kind of proactive.

Keeping a community of people together.

Fostering interesting debates, making sure you got a good network of people there. All that kind of stuff that all helps.

Is it worth people, in your opinion, pursuing education if they want to get into community management or is it much better to just be out there doing it? I mean obviously there's no Community Manager course as such.

No, I don't suppose there is. I guess the closest thing to doing like a formal community management thing would be to do a P.R. or Marketing degree or something like that. Obviously I have a business degree which did have some marketing and stuff included in it so some of that stuff's helpful. So you could perhaps do something like that, but ultimately it's going to be far more important that you do other stuff, that you are responsible for organising tournaments and clans, writing a bit, maybe teaching yourself some web code because that can really help. A lot of community management is about writing out emails using HTML and that sort of thing, all that helps as well.

So what are the best and worst parts of your role?

The best part I think is the Expo, seeing it all come together and seeing loads of gamers come into a room and just have a really great day. That's the best thing for me because I just love seeing people enjoy themselves. The vast majority of those who come to our shows really, really do and you can see that, they just have such a good time and that's the most satisfying for me after all those months of work just to see everyone enjoying themselves is brilliant.

The worst part is sometimes, I've seen this a lot in the last week, since we just re-launched the Eurogamer website, your community will tell you stuff that you don't want to hear, repeatedly and in very angry tones, so be prepared for that. I can imagine that if you're a community manager on a game and that game launches and it's full of bugs there is not going to be a huge amount of fun on the forums and that sort of stuff. So you're going to need a bit of a thick skin in some respects, but I think it's misleading sometimes when you see peoples' reaction on a forum you can kind of get mistaken into thinking that's the mentality of everyone either reading the website or playing the game if you're working on a game, but it would be wrong to think that.

Of course we're in a day and age where everyone has an opinion and method of voicing it.

That's true, but remember that people are far more into and motivated about posting opinions, about being upset about stuff than they are about being happy about stuff. The vast majority of people who play a game and really love it or who read our website and really love it won't post a message on our forum or send us an email saying that. They're far more likely to send us bitchy emails. Don't get too disheartened by that stuff. Always listen to your community, but try and remember that a few people on a forum do not constitute your entire audience.

So we're discussing in the book the pain and joy that is crunch. Do you have much overtime in your role?

Yes. Well there is in the sense that there's always stuff to do, like community management just for the website for example. The forum is always on and it's always active, so there's always stuff going on there. There's always something going on, on Twitter or Facebook, so you do kind of end up monitoring that stuff during most of your waking hours so you could call that overtime I guess. When it comes to Expo organisation there's tons, especially from about July until we start in September. It's working, like basically I'll tend to do 9-5 in the office, but then I'll go home and sit and work most of the evenings during that three month period and I'll do weekend work a lot as well. It's for three months before the Expo that there's that amount of overtime.

And it has to be done for it to be a success.

Yeah. There are two of us who work full-time on the Expo in house and that's it. It's a big event so lots to do you got to do it really.

So another thing we discuss or try to discuss as it's quite a difficult subject is what sort of challenges do women face in a male dominated industry? Any views on that in your previous role or as a Community Manager? Do you think that women still face challenges in the industry? Do you think things have got better?

I think it's clear that women are hugely under-represented in games. I'm not sure if that's because there's endemic sort of sexism or because there are fewer women who are interested, I'm not really sure. At Eurogamer for example we have two women working for us full time out of a full-time staff of about 35 or 40.

So quite representative of the industry then.

Yeah, it's sad. I hope it changes. It should because I think people, whether men or women, whatever background they're from, you need a good mix of people and backgrounds to make interesting games, more interesting content, more interesting websites and stuff like that and I think we still are too focused on the industry being...

Boys with toys.

Yeah, white males 18-35.

That's another interesting thing that was picked up in the Blitz interview... Ethnicity in video games is almost non-existent.

Eurogamer for example is 100 percent white.

In fairness, Brighton in itself tends to struggle with ethnicity.

Yeah, perhaps that's the thing, However, I think people outside that white male 18-35 demographic are underrepresented and I do think it harms the industry. I do think things will be more interesting if you mix things up, new ideas, new angles, that sort of thing.

If you can offer one bit of advice to people starting out on their career, what would that be?

I think it just goes back to something I said earlier. Be lucky and take opportunities when they arise even if they don't look 100 percent right, even if you're unsure. If it looks like it could lead to something else there's no harm in just giving it a go. If you don't take the chance you'll never get there.

Name:	Dan Pearson	*Currently working for:*	Gamesindustry.biz
Age:	31	*Current role:*	Senior Staff Writer
Sex:	Male	*Length of Service:*	15 months

Dan and I met a few years ago when I agreed to do a podcast for Eurogame.net. Since then we've worked together on a career panel discussing routes and roles in the industry. You might have read some of his work on Eurogamer.net or Gamesindustry.biz.

Thanks for agreeing to this interview Dan. We'll start by looking at your career so far. You've been a games journalist now for five years, why did you want to get into the games industry?

I spent the five years or so, up to graduating from university doing horrifically unsatisfying temp jobs. I was constantly looking for jobs I knew that I could get, that was basically my main criteria. Will they employ me? Is it going to pay the rent? Nothing too ambitious but that's was kind of what I wanted to do at the time/what I ended up doing. So I got sick of that one day and started searching (online) for my dream job, which was being a game journalist essentially. I found out there was a job going at Eurogamer (just up the road from me) and I thought what the hell, may as well give it a go and that was kind of how it happened. I think I was just the last person hassling Rupert (C.E.O.) about 2 months later and they took my C.V. and said they'd think about it. I just kept hammering them with emails and he was like: "Right you're the last person to be bothering me still. You clearly want it more than anyone else". So I got the job as web admin, which at the time was essentially uploading a lot of video and screenshots, doing all the stuff no one else wanted to do. So very much starting out on the bottom rung, Eurogamer has always given me the chance to prove myself and eventually I got some writing roles and progressed from there.

Interesting, so what do you actually do in the industry then?

Literally now I'm at Gi which is a trade focused site so I do mostly news and features really, but also I do coordination of stuff for events with companies and things like that. So we'll sort out media partnerships or just arranging stuff with TIGA to get on board with their awards and various other things, so sort of relationship building as well. But day to day it's mostly writing news in the mornings, getting on with features stuff in the afternoons and occasionally getting on with more long term stuff.

So Eurogamer is very consumer focused and Gi.biz is the industry sister side of that. Why did you decide to leave the more video game review aspect for, I guess, writing about the industry?

I had been a staff writer at Eurogamer for about 18 months and I was still doing some of my old web admin duties as well. So it was an opportunity to do a full time writing job where I didn't have to do any of the other stuff, so I'd be a full time writer which is something I wanted to do. At the time if the job had come at Eurogamer, I probably would have chosen that over the trade job to be honest, but now I'd probably never go back to commercial writing. I really enjoy the trade side, you get really good access to everyone. You find out about stuff that you normally wouldn't, people trust you more, they are more open with you because you're not looking for a punchy headline, not that that is Eurogamer's focus at all.

They're not trying to sell their product to you, they're more willing to open up and just chat.

Yeah and it's less of that kind of weird sort of symbiotic relationship that you tend to have between commercial sites and publishers. We just report on the stuff they do and never try to sensationalist stuff and people are more honest with us as a result. But it's great fun, you get to go to all the sort of events and you get to talk to the real high up people and I've really learnt so much about the industry from it. I learnt a huge amount in the first three to four years here, having been a gamer all my life I thought I knew about the industry and found out I knew absolutely sod all and since joining Gi after Eurogamer I found out that I actually still knew sod all. I've just learnt so much more about how the industry works.

So I guess a games journalist is one of those high profile kind of roles in the industry, primarily because it's one that from a very early age as a gamer you're aware of. It's the one that you kind of interact with and are aware of more than any other role in the industry. So what advice would you give people wanting to follow that career path?

Start as soon as you can and don't expect to get any paid work until you've done a lot of stuff for free, either by writing your own blog or by submitting stuff as a member of a forum. I feel a bit hypocritical saying that because I didn't do that. I took the other route of working at the company and then persuading them that you can write. However, I think if you want to start straight off as a journalist then you have got to have a blog with some really good content on it. You've got to be part of active communities. You've got to be known on a couple of forums. You've got to read the site you want to write for every single day, know exactly what their style is and know you can write to their level. Eurogamer gets dozens of submissions every week from people wanting to write for us, ranging from the quite endearing young kids, six year olds, saying they've just played Smurfs and it's amazing, I want to write a review for you, can you give me a job to people who are like 35 and say they have had another career for the last 20 years, they're sick of it, want a change, can they write for us.

I would love for you guys to hire the six year old.

Yeah.

I think that would be a brilliant week.

It was a pretty good review as well.

Eurogamer gets taken over by the kids and just let the kids write for a week about what they want.

That would be awesome, just give the Skyrim review to a seven year old.

So do you feel there's as much competition to be a games journalist as there is to be a developer? Obviously the book talks a lot about the competition around getting into games. I personally would love to write video game reviews, but I've never even contemplated applying to that sort of role because I just think it's going to be far too heavily subscribed.

It is, it is massively, massively competitive. A lot of it is down to luck to be honest. It's about getting that break, but I think if you've got a portfolio of well written stuff then that makes a huge difference. If you just write someone an email saying: "Hey, I play a lot of games. I want to review them". Then they'll just go: "Yeah whatever". However, if you send someone six well written reviews that are all really well written and aimed specifically to that websites style then, at the very least, they'll read all of that and give you decent feedback on what you need to change if you want to write for them. At the best they'll just give you a job, some freelance work. That's the other thing, freelance work is much easier to come by than salary stuff. There are so few salaried games journalist jobs in the country, there's probably fifty. Fifty actually full time game journalists jobs and there are probably five/six hundred freelance jobs I guess.

It kind of mirrors the industry itself.

Yeah. Absolutely!

In terms of temporary and permanent roles, do you think, I mean what is the future of a games journalist? I and this could be my misconception, I've always seen it as perhaps more a young person's role, as games development tends to be, but you know you don't find fifty year old game journalists.

No I think that's partly because you don't find many fifty year old gamers, the medium has kind of matured with its audience. I think fifteen years ago people didn't really write reviews for thirty five year olds, because there weren't any thirty five year old buying games so there's no point. Now the average age is much older.

It's about 32-42

Yeah absolutely, so those are the target audience. Those are the guys that:
a) Websites know are reading their sites and
b) That publishers know are buying their games.

Eurogamer has got an older demographic than I think a lot of sites to be honest, an older probably slightly better read demographic I think and I believe a lot of people read the content for the pleasure of reading it, rather than just as a fact finding experience. I also think to a certain extent that it is a young man's game because it's not very well paid to start off with and usually younger people are much happier with that than the people with mortgages and kids. I didn't join the industry until I was 25/26, so I got in quite late, but I also think that works in your favour as your writing tends to mature. There are not many people who can write extremely well at 21, there are notable exceptions people like Keza MacDonald who has been banging out awesome copy for many, many years now. She's only 23 and now she's the games editor of IGN U.K. so you can do it.

That's phenomenal at such a young age.

Yeah totally, she's been very much a bit of a prodigy. Most of our writers are around 30 or above, people like Simon P, Chris D and Dan W. They have all been playing games for around 25 years, but they're all above 30.

So if you were hiring would you put more emphasis on education or experience?

Experience absolutely one hundred percent, no games editor gives a s**t whether you've got a degree in creative writing. That's completely useless, like it's great that you know how to structure something and that you can use proper devices and things like that, but it's much easier for them to sit and read through a fifteen hundred words review that you've written rather than work out whether you've gone to a decent university and what that's going to teach you and whether you're going to be reliable in the future. If you can prove that you can consistently knock out good copy that is all that matters. You could have come straight from high school and be able to do that and that's all that's going to matter.

Do you have any final thoughts for people hoping to be a games journalist in their future?

Yeah be ready for a lot of knock backs, like I say I feel hypocritical saying this because I got incredibly lucky and managed to just search for the right job at the right time and I was living in the right place.

I actually wouldn't worry it seems to be a prevailing theme, I myself got hideously lucky. Ninety percent of people interviewed in this book got lucky.

Yeah, so I think you've got to be incredibly passionate about it and you've got to really, really want it, but don't get too depressed if it doesn't end up being your career. If it's something you enjoy doing anyway, just keep doing it. Have a blog where you write about stuff and that sort of thing. That can turn into a business as well if you can start to monetise your own blog that makes you a games journalist.

Of course there are many examples within the industry of people who are just fans of the industry and suddenly they become known entities, Penny Arcade, VG Cats, Felicia Day. These are all just people who love gaming and suddenly they're known for it and can even make a buck from it.

Totally and a lot of our freelancers started like that. Chris D for instance was a writer for kids TV I think and he loved games. He was just writing his personal stuff about games and people loved it and said you should try and sell it so, you know, now he does. However, I can imagine it would be very thankless, constantly kind of hammering stuff out and never getting a response, but the fact of the matter is even though its hugely competitive ninety percent of those competitors are not up to standard. So if you do things properly and you are a good writer then you've got a very good chance of getting noticed.

So what is the best and worst thing about your role?

The best thing is basically meeting a huge amount of people that I massively respect. You just have chats to people like Peter Molyneux or you'll meet the head of Activision or I met Richard Bartle who created the whole MMO genre.

There are certain moments that even I, as a bit of a veteran of the industry, remind me of that certain boyhood wow moment. I think my first interview at SEGA was certainly Jesus Christ this is SEGA!! I grew up on their content kind of affair.

Yeah, yeah totally having worked with people whose reviews I read when I was much younger and thinking these guys are awesome, that's fantastic it really is. Having worked with people like Tom and Ollie and Ellie and Matt Martin at Eurogamer, it's a phenomenal place to work because they are the best in the business, so it's fantastic.

The worst part of being a games journalist?

Seeing behind the scenes at the meat factory basically. If you ever went to a meat factory you'd probably never eat another pie and to a certain extent you see a lot of the less pleasant side of the industry. You see all the stories about publishers trying to buy reviews and you see people making threats about advertising if they don't get the right score. You see the petulance and you see the factory floor that is a lot of it, churning out sequels and a lot of the soullessness of it. Completely balanced out by the fact that you see an incredible amount of passion and hope and kind of innovation in it as well, but you do see behind the scenes a little bit and sometimes that does kind of spoil things.

One of the things we touch on in a couple of interviews is, are video games over glamorised?

Yeah! I think that's absolutely right. It's a product you know and I think that's one thing that took me a long time to realise when I started. It is just a business, an industry people are trying to make money out of it and sell things. They're not all sitting in a castle made of dreams and being lovely to each other.

You're more than likely to be working on Barbie's Horse Adventures, Catwoman or Mr Potato Head than you are on Zelda, Master Chief or Gears of War and I guess the same is true for journalism, you're more likely to review noughts and crosses than you are Zelda.

I had written for about 8 months before I reviewed a game I actually enjoyed, it's not a lot of fun. As I'm sure you understand as well from your Q.A. stuff, people get into to that often thinking they're going to be playing amazing games all day and then they end up playing a 30 second loop of something broken and rubbish.

When you do get to work on perhaps one of your favourite titles, as a reviewer, how do you approach that? Are you concerned about being biased because you love the series and you love that studio's output? Or is it really forget you all I get to play my favourite game for the next week and it's a month and a half before it's released?

There's a bit of both, like you never enjoy a game as much when you're playing it for a review, because you don't just sit down and relax, you have to force yourself to play it for 8 hours a day. It doesn't sound like a task, but it's kind of like being forced to eat really nice ice cream for ages, it's great, but you do start feeling a bit sick and wishing you could have just a bit each day. So it does kind of spoil things a bit like that and you do have to be careful of being a bit biased, but at the end of the day if it's all opinion anyway as long as you justify what you're saying and make it clear that's why you like it, I think that's probably fair enough.

Now it's interesting you say that because recently Eurogamer has hit the headlines a bit with a review for Uncharted 3 I believe. I've only glanced at the review, but I've read a lot of the news around it. I think it's quite fair and balanced, but people have been in an absolute uproar about it.

That's the other downside of the job. You always get the most vicious and unpleasant of feedback. It's amazing how emotionally invested people can be in a game and how incredibly vociferously they can voice their opinion about something that they have never played, that you've just spent 14 hours going through and putting your professional opinion on and they will tell you every which kind of unpleasant way that you're absolutely wrong about that.

And they haven't even played it yet!

Yeah "You're being paid by the opposition" or that "you're just trying to ruin people's day by doing this", it is phenomenal. It really is incredible how much viciousness is involved with the feedback for it.

I did an interview for a website a few months ago and I mentioned that I didn't like Gears of War. The campaign's alright, but it just isn't really my cup of tea and I got loads of abuse. It's literally almost a case of your opinion differs from mine and is therefore wrong.

Yeah! Totally.

Of course we're in an age where people are able to get their opinions out when they read something they don't like or disagree with, but it's absolutely crazy what it's been like over that one review.

It's something I really don't miss from commercial stuff. You know you put the score on the end and just having people rip into you for stuff. You have to develop a pretty thick skin quite quickly. I know most reviewers just stop reading the feedback because quite frankly a lot of its really unpleasant and upsetting. Some of the stuff Ellie has had to put up has just been absurd, really, genuinely if someone said that to you in public you probably would just smack them in the face. They are keyboard warriors who would never back it up in person.

Do you think gamers are much harsher to Ellie because of her gender?

Oh without a doubt, absolutely one hundred percent!

Why?

Because a lot of them are a bunch of idiots and assume it's a boys' hobby, their own little club house, no girls allowed. They just see it as their hobby being invaded by women if they're reviewing stuff.

But at the same time could Eurogamer not be accused of perpetuating that themselves? When you and I did the podcast with Ellie she had been reviewing Sorority Life on Facebook.

She had yes.

Which does strike me as kind of giving the girly games to the girl to do?

Well she actually wanted to do that. We hadn't done any reviews of casual games on Facebook at all so we thought we should start. So Ellie volunteered to do that and picked a couple of others as well. It was more just that she wanted to do the feature really, rather than anything else. She's done plenty of girly games as well, she ends up doing a lot of those because she likes a game she can really lay into, basically, which is something she's awesomely good at.

So how does it kind of work? You've got ten titles in the office, does Rupert just hand them out?

It's Martin Robinson who does that now. As the Reviews Editor he works out who is free, which freelancers need work. If someone's particularly invested in a game and really, really wants to do it, they'll get it obviously. Rupert will sometimes weigh in and pull rank and say he's going to do something, but generally it's Martin Robinson who decides.

But it's good that they take your own passion and interests into consideration.

Yeah.

So one thing we touched on a little bit earlier that I'm sure will be of interest to everybody out there. Has any company ever attempted to pay you off?

No, not me personally. It's odd, it's something you hear about happening. We've got a very cast iron policy on it of just absolutely not. However, it does happen, we've had people approach us, probably off the record and I'm certainly not going to say who, but we've had people try and do that, yeah. We've heard from several trustworthy sources that other sites do do it. People literally will sell review scores, whether it's for advertising space, an exclusive, straight up cash or whether it's for a press trip to Malibu for two weeks.

I guess the most known cases are the ones where it's kind of if you do not give this game an eight minimum you will never see another one of our games again.

Oh yeah, we've had people cutting us off all the time. We've had people say we're not picking the phone up to you or we're not sending you any copies of the games and we had to go out to the shop and buy one on release. We're quite open about it, we'll say we haven't reviewed it early because they wouldn't send us one because they're pissed off because we gave their game this or we said this about their game or we didn't give them enough space. It's weird some P.R.s, by all means not all of them, consider that the games press is part of the P.R. industry. So they think that we should just do what we're told, give the game the score we're told and we'll get our copies and our advertising running and that's it, that's the nature of the relationship.

So in essence they see you as almost a subsidiary of their own company?

Yeah, totally. Just an extension of P.R.

So you're there just to promote rather than to critique?

Yeah we're there to push games to the consumer rather than give them informed choices.

So what's the average day like for you?

So I start at 8, which is one of the bad things about the job. You have to do long hours and start early.

Why so early?

Well we have to get the news up, so we want to be able to get four or five news stories up before people read the site, before work.

Before twenty past nine.

Yeah because people will get into work and they'll go through their emails and they will check the site. So yeah I'll get in at eight, wade through emails and then we all work on news usually until lunchtime. Then if someone's got a feature to write up or some transcription to do or another interview to do or some questions to write they'll get on with that and whoever's not busy with those will just keep an eye on the news and keep things ticking over.

And are the bulk of the reviews done in house or is it more a case of you're off to see Ubisoft, you're off to see SEGA?

Well we don't do any reviews on Gi now, but we do features and interviews so we go to see them. Whether that's at events or we go and see them in their offices or we do them over the phone. With reviews generally we used to do much more reviewing actually physically in the office. There were more of us working here who actually reviewed stuff, now the only people who work in the office and review are John Bedford and Tom Bramwell and they tend to do stuff here.

So is everyone else freelance?

Everyone else is freelance or there's Ollie and Martin who work remotely most of the time. Then there's Ellie, she's on maternity leave now, but she works remotely too. Otherwise most of the bulk of it is taken up with freelance and I think that's probably true of most sites to be honest, some more than others, Edge particularly do, they're ninety percent freelance I think, but I think a lot of people use more outsource than in.

So we've discussed in the book the process known as crunch and you've mentioned your early starts, is there a lot of overtime in games journalism?

Yeah there is. So for me it's staying up till ten o clock at night to do the American financials or getting up at six in the morning to do the Japanese financials or going to an event somewhere and doing a twelve, thirteen hour day just because you have to cover everything or doing networking and things like that, so there is a fair bit and you know you do what it takes to get it done. The hourly rate tends to not be brilliant because the wages aren't amazing, but they're better here than most other places I think in terms of journalism.

What sort of wage range could a games journalist expect?

I know a lot of people who work on print are starting off, I mean, they're starting now saying you've got to do a year internship before you get a job. However, there are people who are starting on eleven thousand and working forty five hour weeks.
So what can you expect that to move on to?

It depends who you work for. I know that we've had people join us who have been writing for five or six years, who have had quite senior positions and have joined us as staff writers they've had a wage rise of three or four grand and they've literally left a five year career having been paid less than eighteen grand a year.

Absolutely crazy, as we said earlier it's one of the more visible roles in the industry so you do expect it to be not necessarily amazingly well paid but...

I think it's a hang up of the fact that there were so many people to do it, who wanted to do it that until quite recently it wasn't really a professional money making thing.

Very similar to Q.A. where so many people want to do it and therefore you can keep wages at a certain minimal rate.

Absolutely, you can expect to be starting on a minimum wage.

So another thing we touch on in the book is the gender make up of the industry and how no matter what side you fall on it will impact on your working life. Do you have any thoughts about the challenges women may face in the industry and do women face any challenges or is it a non-existent issue?

I think certainly in the journalism side they probably do, not from the employers, but from the audience.

We've already discussed some of the more horrible comments one of your colleagues has had to put up with.

Yeah there are some very high profile female journalists. There's obviously Ellie and we've spoken about Kezza and Rachel Weber who works for us, she was OPM news editor for a long time, then there are people like Leigh Alexander. There are some very prominent female writers. I don't know whether the lower numbers reflect the fact that fewer women want to do it, I think that's probably at least part of it. We certainly get fewer applications from women, but I think there are women who are getting much more negative feedback from their audiences. I don't think in any way that any employer would judge a potential employee on their gender but I would think that women are much more likely to be put off when they do start writing because they get disregarded by a lot of people who assume that they don't know what they're talking about.

So would you say that women do need to work harder certainly in games journalism to prove themselves to the audience rather than the employers?

Yeah I'd of said so because you know what it's like, put any comments anywhere and people always pick up on the easiest thing to lay into. As we've said most comments are negative, they will always pick the easiest thing and if that happens to be the fact that a person is a woman then you know that's what they'll start with. I mean we've got a lot of female readers, but they tend to be less vocal, they keep their heads below the parapet, for good reason. It's not really a surprise, but I think there's no gender inequality from employers, I really don't. I don't know what it's like on the development side perhaps it's a bit more pronounced. You do hear some pretty awful stories about some of it and there is a very strong underlying level of almost subconscious sexism in that whenever you go to a games show there are booth babes and whenever you see games artwork there will be a man basically dressed as a tank and a woman in a leather bikini.

But then is that sexism or is it that sex sells? Certainly if you look at perhaps Golden Axe box art you had a woman in a scantily clad bikini, but at the same time you had a bare-chested six pack barbarian. Is it just that sex sells or are we all perverted men?

I think it's probably a little bit of both to be honest. I think female images in games are definitely more sexualised and as you say that's probably because it does sell because the audience are men essentially. So I don't think it's a consciously kind of done thing, but then you also hear stories about the stuff at Techland. They left in a bug and it was basically a derogatory term and you do hear things like the guys at Granger Games* and the GMA's (not a great advert for them), but everyone was outraged which was a good sign that the industry is changing.

*If you're not aware of the recent GMA awards and their sponsor check out what happened here http://www.gizmodo.co.U.K./2011/10/how-an-unknown-games-retailer-committed-suicide-at-a-gaming-awards-event/

So if you could change one thing in the games industry what would it be?

That's tricky, perhaps for it to be less ridiculed in general society and that is something that's really happening now. Even I, as someone who loves video games and who talks about them professionally all the time and understands that there is a lot of very intelligent people involved in them and a lot of subtlety to them, I find it kind of embarrassing when someone who's not really into games starts asking me about games, when people ask what's your favourite game or what have you been playing? Even when I sit there and go: "I've been playing this game where you have to save the world from giant detergent, cotton buds or whatever" it makes you feel like a bit of a child to be honest, whereas if I said "Oh yeah, I've just been watching a Schwarzenegger film" or something equally as ridiculous that would make me feel less of an idiot. So it's weird. I don't know whether that's self imposed and whether the fact that people who don't play games are asking me about them is a sign that they are taken more seriously than I expect them to be. There was a piece on Radio Four this morning, a couple of guys were talking about whether games were art and that kind of thing and it was being taken quite seriously by the Radio Four presenter and that's great, but it's definitely still an anomaly and that's probably more driven by the fact that games make a lot of money than anything else.

But you can easily look at comic books and they're still an industry that's struggling to be deemed as anything other than something kids do. You have some phenomenal authors who write comic books and some amazing artwork. I've lost count of the amount of articles that discuss why when we take something as glorious as writing and something as amazing as art and we put them together does it become something childish and immature?

Exactly, couldn't agree more.

So I guess any final piece of advice for any budding games journalist out there?

Just keep plugging away, keep plugging away and build a good portfolio. Make sure that you're good enough because it's a high standard now whereas it wasn't always, but it is a very high standard right now. Know the industry inside out, be prepared to back up your opinions, don't be a fan boy and just listen to the advice you get, listen to the feedback. If you send someone a piece of writing and they are good enough to tell you what's wrong with it, don't then just get in a huff or a sulk and go: "Well I tried really hard with that", listen to what they've got to say because you'll never get better advice than that.

Excellent advice, thanks for your time Dan.

It's been a pleasure.

Name:	James Grant	Currently working for:	Eurogamer & Gi.biz
Age:	34	Current role:	H.R. Services Manager
Sex:	Male	Length of Service:	6 Months

I've known James Grant for many years. In his previous role as an industry recruitment agent he's found me more work than all the other agencies combined. With such a strong knowledge of the recruitment process, I was keen to hear what he had to say, but to begin with we discussed his current role.

So what is a H.R. Services Manager?

It basically means that I do all the stuff between editorial and sales to do with making the website a service to the industry whether it be H.R. issues like recruitment and stuff or more generally the games industry dot biz network which is like a social network for the games industry.

How long have you been working in the industry?

I've been doing this job for six months, but I've been doing recruitment in the games industry for probably ten years now.

Why did you want to get into the games' industry?

I've always been a gamer, always wanted to be involved with games, but didn't really know how to do that. I don't make any games, I don't programme, I don't make any art or design games, but I like playing with them/playing them. So I started off doing recruitment basically and after a while decided to get some game industry clients by just phoning them up out of the blue

So this was off your own back, nothing your boss had said about getting into the games industry market. You just thought people work in games, let's see if there's a market here.

Yeah, more specifically, I was working in the City, in early 2000, doing recruitment for the City then the dot com bubble burst and all those websites that were worth a lot of money suddenly weren't worth anything so they weren't recruiting. Banks similarly struggled. Then September 11th 2001 happened and all our bank clients stopped recruiting and I'm sitting there with a sales target to hit as a recruiter!

And no one to recruit for....

And no one to recruit for. However, we had a lot of bright, high-calibre graduates and junior staff from Imperial, Cambridge, Oxford, those sorts of places, with First Class degrees, 2.1s even maybe, straight A's at A levels who had done some C++ and general programme work and perhaps done their dissertation in 3D programming or something cool and had thought, well I want to get into banking because that's kind of the industry to get into. I just phoned up some companies like Criterion, the guys that make Burn Out, they made Renderware which is a rendering engine so they would have been very technical people. I just phoned them up and said I have some bright clients, what about it? They took my C.V.s and I started getting those sorts of games clients.

So it kind of just rolled from there?

Yeah because of circumstance, because of the situation I found myself in. I thought well let's just phone up some companies I know, because I knew about games as a consumer and could therefore at least have a vaguely credible conversation with the people who answer the phone and the managers and stuff.

Was it easy to get your way in or were the shutters down and the barriers up? Did you find these people quite easy to approach?

I think they're easy to approach if you treat them professionally and don't make a fool of yourself. If I was just another numb-nuts recruitment consultant then they probably wouldn't have been that interested. I just handled myself professionally and had some decent candidates.

So it's down to your approach and the quality of your portfolio of clientele.

Yeah and candidates. It's also purely down to me just sitting there and going how am I going to make money that month, hit my sales target? So I just picked up the phone to some companies. Burnout had just come out and that was a very good game, Burnout 1, back in 2001/2002, when Acclaim published it.

It must have gone well because obviously a few years later, a young tester with a gleam in his eye contacted a certain recruitment agent and we discussed potential roles for the first time and by that point you were solely doing games recruitment were you not?

Yeah, so basically then you steamroll it. Once you get Criterion as a client, you then get KUJU as a client and then Argonauts. Then you can phone up EA or anyone and say "I've got this client base with these other companies" and you build up your own client base. As long as you're not annoying anyone or losing any of those clients, you build up your own client base. Of course, then the banking recruitment company that I worked for said "O.K., so banks are now recruiting again" as these things all work in cycles. They said come back and recruit for Merrill Lynch and Goldman Sachs again. They look for the same person over and over again, straight A's, First Class degree, middle class guys, it's very dull kind of recruitment, whereas in the games industry you've got programmers, artists, designers, Q.A. people, there's a much more wider range.

Not forgetting the roles themselves. From time to time unusual and quite interesting roles come up.

Yep, varied absolutely. I ended up leaving that company and joining a very small agency that had a little games' desk run by a guy called Stewart Godfrey, who is now a Recruitment Manager at Climax. Stewart and I worked together for a good couple of years and then Argonauts was one of my clients and that's when I spoke to you. So I never really set out to be in the games industry, but when push comes to shove I was like "I will see how this goes" and ten years later I still am.

So due to a love of games it sprung to mind as an opportunity to do some sales?

Yeah it's like, when your back's to the wall, what are you going to do? You go to what you know, your hobby or your interests or your passion and I was fortunate enough, I suppose. At the time it was a bit of a random sequence of events, with hindsight I like to think that I was intelligent enough to combine my hobby with my career, which is quite rare you know, a rare opportunity.

Certainly a lot of the interviews, even the ones we've done today, discuss luck as being a part of it. I always thought that I just lucked into video games. Many other people I've chatted to kind of have the same idea. Again, luck is one thing, but it's what you do with the opportunity that comes along.

Yeah. I could have picked up the phone to Criterion or KUJU or Argonauts and not handled myself correctly or not done what needed to be done as a recruiter and I would have come across as a bit of a fan boy, timewaster. There's still a job to be done and whether the games industry is cool or not and whether it's an aspiration place to work or not, there's still a professional job to be done.

Do you think the games industry is over glamorised?

Yeah, absolutely, because ultimately it comes down to hard work and long hours. You need to be good at your job

The fact is it is a job.

Yeah it is a job and to be fair the games industry clients I had were just clients who I would send C.V.s to and make placements at and that was all great. It was a value added thing on top of that, it was a nice thing as well that I had a vague interest in the products that they were making. It was quite cool, but it was very, very fortunate that I was able to combine those two. However, it's still going to be down to me being a good recruitment consultant at the end of the day.

So how did you go from industry recruitment to your current role?

I think just because recruitment consultancy and recruitment agents in the games industry provide a certain service to the industry, I'd say quite a limited service, a lot of companies recruit directly themselves. A lot of people apply to companies directly and the agencies are there to bridge that gap. However, agencies can be accused of being surplus to requirements or not being a key part of the industry.

A necessary evil?

A necessary evil would be a good phrase yeah. The good guys are well known and the bad guys are well known as well. It's a very one dimensional job. You get a good C.V., you put it forward for a job and you forward the job and that's kind of it. However, there's a whole wider area of getting guys jobs in the games industry, in a broader sense. So whether it be through education, through this kind of project that you're doing, through the game jobbers career fair, at the Euro Gamers Expo at Earls Court, whether it be having a good job board where a company's going to advertise their jobs and people can apply for those jobs, there's a whole kind of services ecosystem around getting a job in the games industry that needed our attention. Certainly Gamesindustry.biz is a website I'd used for 8 years as a recruiter and thought it was always excellent as a recruitment tool, as a job board, I thought what would be better than to go in-house at that place and actually make the website better. Better at getting guys jobs in the industry through the job board, through education, through events and through this kind of thing. So my job is applying my ten years of recruitment experience in a sort of sandbox environment, kind of like think that would work or that wouldn't or I think this feature would be good or I think this event would be good or I think this initiative would be good.

Do you think that a part of the recruiter's role, certainly when dealing with, perhaps, junior or fresh new candidates, is dispelling the myth?

Yeah that's all very well, but the reality is that as a recruiter your job is commercially driven, so you're not targeted or you're not motivated to spend that time educating people as to how to get a job on a one to one basis. That was the interesting thing about the shift to what I'm doing now which is my job is actually about...

Engaging those candidates?

Yeah, engaging with those people because if I'm a recruitment consultant with a target to hit, with a sales target to hit or with that very short term commercial agenda, I'm not going to spend my time talking to guys who have just graduated with a 2.2 with a poor portfolio. I'm not going to spend half an hour on the phone to him because it's a waste of my time.

Is it worth these people getting in touch with recruitment agencies when they've just finished education or is it a case that they should try and build up some experience first?

Well I think it's too late by that point. I think recruitment agencies are very good at getting you a job once they've got something to work with. If they've got nothing to work with, if you're not bringing anything to the table, if you've got nothing to offer either an employer or recruitment agency, in terms of what they can put you forward for, then there's not much they can do for you, so it's up to you.

Well, you've done your programming or your art or design degree.

If all you've done is turn up and get a degree, then there's nothing you're doing that makes you stand out from the crowd. So the things you need to be doing are getting a portfolio, doing extracurricular work, doing over and above your course.

Doing Beta tests, making sure your show reel is the best it can be

Make sure you have a great website. If you're a programmer, make sure you have a website with the source code on it. If you're an artist have your portfolio on the website, just make it very accessible, really easy for these guys to have a look at your work.

Because there's hundreds of thousands of other people applying!

Absolutely and if you haven't got those basics things in place by the time you speak to someone like me or certainly a recruitment agency, if they're not seeing those things that day, there's nothing to talk to you about. It's too late by that point certainly from a recruiter point of view. What you need to be doing is thinking a year or two, or even three, in advance what course you're choosing, why are you choosing that course?

What would it lead to?

Yeah, absolutely because I can phone up a company and tell them why I think you'll be a good employee, but if I've got ten candidates like you, if I've got twenty candidates like you, if I've got a hundred candidates like you, why would I waste my time on you? If you think about it, if I spend ten minutes with you, I had a hundred candidates that week, ten minutes times by 100 people that's my entire week gone just giving out free advice to people who are perhaps already too late to the party.

At the end of the day you've got to put bread on the table and feed yourself.

That's why there's a focus on recruitment agencies focusing on experienced candidates because they can do more with those candidates. Equally, as I've gained more experience of the industry I see that the important part of that whole conversation is 2, 3, 4 years before that stage, the sort of stage where you're choosing your courses, making your educational choices so by the time you get to apply for those jobs you're already a bit more street smart than the average candidate, you already know what people look for. I think by the time you get to me it's too late, like I said it's a bit one dimensional because you're either a good candidate for me or you're not and if you're not I can't really help you. But ten years later it would be nice to make more of a contribution. Basically that's why this job working with Gamesindustry.biz and Eurogamer enables me to actually inform more, engage more and give these people more opportunity to apply for the kind of jobs that I couldn't really help them with as a recruitment agency.

So now it's all about helping others or at least a certain amount of it is about helping them, improving the calibre of candidates we see coming into the industry every year.

Yeah and equally if there's less jobs to apply for in a downturn or if there's any challenges like that, then it's not that there's less chance of getting employed it just means that you need to be better, you need to be a better candidate.

You need to raise your bar

You need to raise your game because there's less opportunities out there, so they won't just hire people for the sake of it or they won't hire people to put bums on seats because I think certainly where the industry is heading now, it's less about bums on seats and making big budget next gen games, it's a lot more about smaller, more quality teams. They still want to hire junior candidates, but they're not going to hire ten of them at once, they're going to hire one really good person rather than eight more average people. So each individual needs to be better as a candidate and I think that's about being well informed and a bit more street smart.

Just going back to your career itself, what's good and bad about being a recruiting agent for the industry?

I think the good thing is you can actually make a difference to games and companies, so for example, there are games that have come out, where I look at the credits and go, I know half the programming team, half the art team, a couple of guys on the Q.A team. You think to yourself, do you know what, had I not found that candidate, or had I not made that introduction, then I know that potentially the game would still have come out, but it's nice that you've made that contribution.

So indirectly you've contributed to the game, by contributing to the people who contribute to the game.

Yeah exactly and it's being that middle man, being that kind of enabler, playing that kind of job. As I say, when I go back to the beginning, I don't make games, I'm not a programmer or an artist and I never pretended I ever could be, but that means that my only job therefore would be in those more peripheral kind of roles and responsibilities, so being a bit of a matchmaker in a company. Like a company's making a really good action adventure game, they need really good characters so by finding a really strong character artist for that team you know that character you're playing with was modelled by the candidate that you put into that job it's just quite cool.

But then it must be rewarding finding people find work anyway?

I think that's balanced by, that's when you get into the negative side, that's balanced by the fact that for every 100 applications you can only help 2.

So that's 98 you have to say no thanks to, which is pretty hard

But for different reasons sometimes, so for example 5 or 10 of those might not be right this time, but they might be right in a year's time or two years time or for a different job.

They may need some more experience first

Yeah exactly, so I might not have a job at that time for that person, but maybe in 6 months time I do. It's trying to be positive with everybody, but ultimately it's trying to be realistic with people as well. So yeah every time it works out, every time that 1, 2 candidates do get that job there are literally tens of people that you are having to, not let down, but not disappoint

Dishearten?

Well that's the thing. I think it's how then you communicate that with them. I think that's the other frustration about being a candidate when you're dealing with an agency, if you don't hear anything back (If you apply for a job and you hear nothing back). I think it's important to try, I'm being realistic, I think it's important to try to contact candidates and say these are the reasons why.

Otherwise how would the candidate hope to improve?

But then we get into the realms of it's not my job to make your career better by me giving you advice. I try to give relevant feedback, but again if you're not doing the basic things, getting a good degree hopefully, having a good portfolio, having a website, you know, doing those basic things, I'm not going to hold your hand through the feedback process that I'm spending time on. However if you're a decent candidate, I'm going to tell you why you've come up short that time. Usually it's down to being in the wrong place at the wrong time, rather than being at the right place at the right time. So that's what I would say is the downside about being an agent, is it's a roller-coaster ride. It is like great things can happen one day, really frustrating and annoying things can happen another day. Because that can affect your bottom line, it can be quite an emotional roller-coaster, certainly that's the frustration. Another highpoint was getting a production credit on Catwoman, on EA's Catwoman in 2004. That was quite cool, it was nice getting a credit on a game.

So, if hiring would you put more emphasis on education or experience?

I would say talent is the word you'd probably use and that's probably a combination of both. So if you're talented then you'll have a good portfolio irrelevant of the academic experience you've got. If you have lots of experience, but you've been working on subpar games, doing subpar work, then yeah you've got the three years experience, but your art work isn't very good or your portfolio isn't very good. So you can have lots of experience and not be very good and you can have no experience and be very good, so I think it comes down to is that talent is the deciding factor which is why I think it's very frustrating for candidates. It's like you're either good at your job or you're not, but that's the reality of getting a job in the real world, right? You can't go on and be a games artist and be proper rubbish.

No matter what it is you will always have people who are faster, far smarter and better able than you, but that's not to say you have to slump into a rut and give up.

So there is that element of the X Factor, Britain's Got Talent kind of situation, where people are just awful, but in that sense the best thing to do is just tell people you haven't got the talent.

That must be harsh to tell someone.

But that's the point, if it's not me that's telling them who is. If Simon Cowell doesn't say, sorry chief you can't sing for toffee, he's not doing them a favour. He's doing it in a very unkind way, but just because you've done a degree from a university in games programming, it doesn't mean you're entitled to a job in games programming. Much like getting a job in computer science or an accountancy qualification doesn't entitle you to be an accountant, it qualifies you. It's some bit of paper, but it doesn't mean you're a good accountant. So it's the same in any kind of walk of life. So I think what it comes down to isn't experience of academics, it's the talent to do the job. How you get that experience is the age old question and I think being in the right place at the right time is an important part of that. Again a lot of people will look at your portfolio and if it's good it will catch people's eye, it will catch my eye, it will catch the art director's eye and it will catch the lead artist's eye. If it's not very good, it won't. So maybe when you say:"Oh I've applied for loads of jobs. I've not heard anything back, or how do you get experience when I haven't got any experience?" well if you're not catching the Pope's eye the reality is there's potentially a reason for that. What I'm interested in is the other type where you've got a candidate who is clearly talented, who clearly knows what he's doing, clearly has something, but maybe hasn't presented themselves as best they could in their portfolio or they've done a course but it's a bit of a poor course, they haven't really got much out of it, but you can see something there, maybe they've got a great demo. They've got a 2.2 (from university) in Games Technology, from some company but the demo's actually quite awesome. Well, what's the reason for that, maybe the course didn't inspire them, but the demo's good, there's obviously some talent there. So as I say, if you've got the talent you will get people's attention. The system does work.

One of the things that was touched upon when I went to interview Blitz Games was that some candidates leave their coding or art or design or even Q.A. course, almost expect that because they've done the course we have to hire them

Yeah.

Almost like it's a given right away that because they've done the course that instantly translates into a job. One of the hard things I'm sort of struggling with communicating in this book is that if you're truly passionate, you work hard, you have a bit of luck and you do the right things then yes you can break into the industry. However, it's highly competitive and just doing a course means nothing

Yeah. It's like doing any sort of creative course. It's like doing a course in creative writing. Doesn't mean you're going to get your novel published.

So do people have unrealistic expectations about entering the industry after studying? Do they believe that just because they've studied they're entitled to a job in the industry?

If you do a course in games design or game programming or game art or anything like that, it doesn't entitle you to a job in that role. It's like doing a course in anything, be it, accountancy or anything like that, that you've done a qualification in it doesn't mean you're entitled to a job. You've got to be good at what you're doing and when you talk about all the different jobs that you can do in the games industry, around the games industry, whether it be sales, marketing, community management, recruitment, whatever you need to be good at those jobs first or have the talent for those jobs first and then you might get a job doing it. Just because you've got a degree in it or done a course in it, doesn't mean you're going to get a job in that. That's where it comes down to your portfolio and how you present yourself as well because ultimately that's two extreme cases. Either you've got the talent to do or you haven't, but in the middle there's the element of if you can be a bit more well presented, be a bit more street-smart about it and present yourself in a better way then it might get you that foot in the door, but just having a course in that subject doesn't get you in the door. It might be a good foundation, but it doesn't entitle you to that and I think that's the problem people have because ultimately, yeah, they could do a different course, say in computer science, rather than games programming and even if they don't get a job in that games role, they can obviously fall back on doing something else.

So one of the things we discuss is potentially the challenges women face in the games industry, it is after all a male dominated industry. Do you think perceptions are changing? Do you think the challenges are all made up? Do you think that there are real challenges that women have to face?

I don't know. It's a difficult one. Certainly in my ten years I've probably helped like one female programmer get a job and maybe three or four game artists. You're probably looking at like one percent of the placements I've made or dealt with, but it's just one of those things. I think that gaming is a male dominated entertainment. The games are very much male orientated.

We're talking about the industry that didn't even see females as a consumer until relatively recently.

If we go back to why people get into the games industry, it's because they love games. They like games. The games industry isn't obliged to be a job that appeals to men and women. It just so happens that the subject matter of a lot of games you're working on is male orientated whether they be racing games or shooting games, whatever. From an employment point of view they're obviously entitled to be an equal opportunities employer, but if (out of the applicants they get), they get 50 applicants and one is female, that's just the reality of who's applying for it you know. You can't have positive discrimination because that's largely pointless. If they're not talented for the job then they won't be the best candidate. The reality is a lot of game design studios are purely male, however interestingly enough when you look at H.R. managers, a lot of support staff, a lot of general sort of reception staff, in terms of H.R. managers I would probably say 90 percent are female. The recruitment manager(s) maybe it's a bit more 50/50. However, speak to an H.R. manager at a games company and 9 times out of 10 they're female, but those people aren't there because of video games, they're there because it's an H.R. job or they're a receptionist because it's a receptionist job or whatever their job is. Yeah, when you look at the core games job it is predominately male orientated, but I think there are probably quite a few artists and animators who are female. It's just one of those situations where the subject matter you're working on is predominately male orientated, whereas some studios, I'm thinking of Relentless down here in Brighton who make games like Buzz and more family orientated games, certainly I know a couple of programmers there that are female, a number of designers that are female, a number of artists that are female.

So it could depend very much on the studio output. If they are predominately after families and social games they do well to have more equal makeup of staff

Absolutely and you need that on the team. If you're 100 percent male it would be difficult to have that diversity that informs your game design. I just think it's one of those things where 90 percent of your consumers are male it's not a surprise that potentially that many of your employees are as well. You could look at the film industry or T.V. industry, but then you could argue that the film and T.V. industry have more of a rounded audience potentially.

If you could change on things in the games industry what would it be?

I think maybe stability's the main thing that springs to mind. It's such a boom and bust industry. You spend two years on a game and it totally tanks in retail and potentially the whole studio is out of a job. Equally you make a game, it does really well and the industry makes ten versions of that game, then that style of game gets over saturated and they stop selling again. When you think about something like Call of Duty, something like that.

Guitar hero?

Rock Band, Guitar Hero was a breakout hit. It came out of nowhere

5-6 years later everyone's sick of it.

Because it got over saturated to an extent where companies that had been bought for 100s of millions of dollars were basically being closed down or being sold for a nominal amount back to the management which is bonkers. Obviously in the mean time the big publisher, Activision, whoever, made money out of it, so everyone's a winner, but yeah it's a very boom and bust sector. People mistake that for potentially a problem. I think from an employment standpoint it's a problem. You want to get a job and you want to stay in it, but that's the nature of any creative industry whether it's T.V. or film.

Just out of curiosity, do you think that out of your time in the industry you've seen more of a move towards temp contracts over permanent roles?

Everyone talks about that, but I don't believe we've seen a big shift, maybe recently. But no, I think it's always been a predominately permanent contract industry, but permanent, like I said before, doesn't always mean much if your company goes bankrupt. I think it would be a lot more realistic if you were on some sort of contract that was related to the project you were working on. Saying you're on a 30 grand a year permanent contract is fine, but if the company goes bust it won't be worth much.

It's worth as much as a temp contract.

Exactly, but you don't see companies wholly contract employee because you want that core culture, that core kind of company ethos.

They have skills they want to retain from one project to the next.

Exactly, what you end up having is a core of permanent staff. So like 50 percent of the team is permanent, they're your guys, they're the guys that know all about your system, who have been trained up and know their stuff. When you need bums on seats in terms of just doing some art, game art or Q.A .or you outsource that to an outsource company. Yeah, it's always been a permanent employment industry and the whole idea of it going more towards a film model is an interesting discussion, but I don't think it would ever happen.

Not something you've seen on the ground?

No, because, again, at most it comes down to the core team being 50 percent permanent, maybe there's some flex and some...

Give and take...

There's some give and take by certain companies KUJU for example or others have that model of a lot of people on contract. Say with SEGA Q.A. a lot of guys are on contracts, but the department...

The core management team...

The core team, even the lead testers, are on contracts. So they're like I don't really care if people turn up late, the cultures a bit crap or if things are slipping in terms of the company and the culture because I'm only here for the next few months potentially. So you need that permanent skeleton, you need a permanent investment, permanent stability.

Because that way your staff buy into your company...

Yeah and actually build a company. So there's always that balance, but yeah, the nature of game development is that you are, as a company, contracted to make your games and deliver on a date.

Another thing I struggle to dispel in the book is that it is a business. The bottom line is money and as much as we'd love to make games and love what we do, we are a business.

Exactly and as a gamer you know that for every game that you play that's awesome, that's phenomenal, there are six games that you don't pick up off the shelf. A game you don't pay attention to, that gets 5 out of 10 on Eurogamer, that aren't worth the paper they're written on, but someone paid to make that game, someone delivered it. The game isn't quality, but maybe that's because it's a tie in with a film, tie in with a T.V. show.

Or it's not marketed at you

Yeah, like Zumba Fitness dominated the charts over the summer because the whole games industry doesn't release games in the summer for some reason and Zumba Fitness obviously caught onto the fitness craze that was sweeping the nation and Zumba Fitness was literally number 1 for 14 weeks, but I wouldn't have brought that ever. Obviously they've made a decent ton of money out of it. If you want to work in the games industry, you could find yourself on a six month contract, working on some random game like Barbie's Horse Adventures or you could find yourself on a six month contract with unsecured employment, working on a game you have no interest in, working on an art style that you have no passion for.

This comes back to being a professional. If you're a designer on My Little Pony, Barbie Horse Adventures or something that you have no interest in, it's down to your professionalism to get interested in that subject.

It comes down to you need to be good at your job and if you're not enjoying that sort of thing you might as well go and be an accountant or a programmer in a bank.

The likelihood is you won't be working on the games you love.

You're not going to be working on Uncharted, you're not going to be working on Batman, Modern Warfare or whatever it is because that's one in a hundred shot isn't it?

Just finally and I'll let you get back to what you do, if you could offer one piece of advice to someone starting out in the industry what would that be?

It would be, be good at your job. Present yourself well. Be professional in it. When I say, be good at your job that starts with choosing what you want to do. I always knew that I enjoyed games, but I never once sat there as a fourteen year old saying I want to be a recruiter in the games industry, but then again I never kidded myself that I could be an artist, or thought I could be a programmer. I tried to learn C, but I was utterly appalling at it. So I'm never going to be a programmer.

At least you tried. You explored that avenue to see if it was one worth pursuing.

I can't draw, I can't programme, I'm quite a good organiser, so I could have been a producer, but I didn't know anyone who would get me into that.

We're talking about a time pre internet. Did anyone know producers existed?

Yeah. Producers didn't really exist back then. The producer role didn't really turn up until like PS2, when budgets started going up, team sizes got bigger, that wasn't even really a job back when I started, but yeah, you need to pick the right job, be good at what you're doing because you're making the right choice, be realistic and then whatever it is you choose, try getting experience doing that, not just in the games industry but generally. If you're a programmer, be a programmer. If you're an artist, get a good portfolio or even do web design or some kind of art related thing or if you want to do community management or recruitment, be a moderator. If you want to be a journalist write. Only then will your talent come through and off the back of that you can start getting people's attention. If you're not very good at your job, if you're not very good at your chosen role or chosen talent, whatever, you want to be don't rely on a course to get you that attention. If you are talented and if you are doing the right course and you do the right things to get yourself a portfolio, to get yourself noticed, then you should actually get noticed. It should work out, if you're any good.

Name:	Bill Stone	**Currently working for:**	Myself
Age:	30	**Current role:**	Sole trader of videogames
Sex:	Male	**Length of Service:**	11 months

Bill used to test for me before deciding he wanted to create and run his own company. Unusually he decided on selling games which gives him a unique insight on games creation from the very start right through to the point of sale.

Why did you want to get into the games industry?

Games have fascinated me from an early age and one of my enduring fantasies from those times was the thought that I could one day be involved in the making of one. I'm not sure it even mattered what exactly, my involvement would be!

How long have you worked in the industry?

Including my time as a Q.A. tester, I would say my involvement in the videogames business has hit 6 years in total.

Who have you worked for in the industry?

Before striking out on my own, I was working for Zoe Mode (formerly Kuju Brighton), where I remained for my entire five year career in games development.

What do you do in the industry?

After achieving what I set out to do and gotten involved in games development via Q.A., I've now sort of moved to the periphery, trading finished games as my own business.

What led you to leaving the creation side of the industry for a retail endeavour?

Having spent my entire career in Q.A. and having no serious desire to move into other roles, I was starting to find the regular threat of redundancy was getting to me. Given how I couldn't see the likelihood of job security getting better anywhere else, my options basically boiled down to sticking with Q.A. at the studio or leaving the industry. When I began to set up the business, my enthusiasm towards becoming self-employed and providing my own security quickly led to me choosing the latter.

What would you say is the highlight of your career so far?

Having had the opportunity to work on a game that was both interesting to me and demonstrated a greater amount of innovation than was typical of the studio at the time. It was easily the most rewarding time of my career as it allowed me to invoke some of the passion I imagined when thinking about the industry in my youth.

So what would you consider the lowlight of your career so far?

This would probably have been a period of time where I was working on a number of what I felt were derivative uninspiring titles while being under near-constant threat of redundancy. It was very difficult to remain motivated in those circumstances

That's interesting. Why do you feel studios bother with unoriginal, uninspiring titles? Or was it just not a title which appealed to you?

I would think it's because there is often little alternative that doesn't involve slashing their workforce drastically while pursuing a creative vision of their choosing. I suppose there'll always be a difference of opinion about what titles are truly uninspiring to work on though. I'm willing to believe not everyone shared my views at my own studio as to which titles were worthwhile creative endeavours and which were purely a means of paying the bills.

How did you originally get into the industry and did you do anything unique to increase your chances?

I was somewhat lucky in this respect. Being unemployed at the time, I was doing some voluntary work to help with job skills when I mentioned my interest in getting in the industry to a careers adviser. They assisted me in tracing the relevant companies in the area and in offering my services for free as a means of getting my foot in the door. As it happened, a games developer was needing hands to test a game of theirs that had just entered the Beta stage and took me on for three months during which time I had the opportunity to prove myself as a tester to the point where I was offered a paid contract at the end of my free period, which I took.

Working for free must have been very hard, yet the final payoff (of a job) quite rewarding. Would you advise this method to others?

It's probably still one of the most effective ways to get inside an industry that is never short of people queuing up for entry-level roles in it. I'd recommend offering your services for free once or twice if you can afford to, as even if no job offer is forthcoming the notch on your C.V. should prove useful when pursuing opportunities for paid work (not to mention giving you a little taste of what you're getting yourself into). Actually getting a job offer was of course a fantastic result for me, but I have a feeling that's not such a common occurrence. The impression I got was that most companies would view voluntary workers as unpaid in-house Beta testers and would have no expectation of hiring them once their agreed voluntary period came to a close.

How did you get into your current role?

I had taken an interest in trading games towards the end of my time in my previous role and began testing the waters by buying a few titles to trade while still in my job. I did this for around two months before deciding this is what I would rather be doing and handed in my notice soon after.

Was it hard to set out on your own? What sort of challenges did you face?

It was certainly daunting, thinking of willingly trading in my status as a paid employee for a future employment that I was solely responsible for. There was a fair amount of self-doubt about whether what I had done was entirely wise, especially after the initial euphoria of having done so had died down. The main challenge that has concerned me since going down this route was ensuring the business was profitable enough to withdraw a reasonable income from before my savings were exhausted. Building up a good online reputation from nothing was something of a poser for me too initially. Other than that, it's just been the trial and error of learning as I go, getting a better feel for what tends to sell and what tends to sit there gathering dust on the shelf.

What advice would you give to people looking to be a trader of videogames in the industry?

Get a feel for the market first by picking up a few cheap games you're confident of selling on for more, then experiment with a venue (EBay, Amazon Marketplace, car boot etc.) to sell them on. Forget about selling the latest releases, as competition is far too fierce and the value of new games depreciate at an alarming rate. Also, remember that if you do decide to start trading games for profit you will need to register with the HMRC as self employed, as any income you make from this will need to be declared to them.

What's the worst thing about your role?

Probably the lack of human interaction that is typical for all home-based occupations. Having a bad week sales wise can put you on a downer too.

So what's an average day for a trader of videogames like?

I'll generally check the latest videogame software prices in the morning, as well as make the bulk of my stock purchases. Early afternoon is spent packaging orders taken for the day and dispatching them to customers, whilst the rest of the afternoon is generally split between emailing customers, checking for pricing updates and putting up sales listings for any new stock delivered during the day.

So what are the longest hours you've worked during a crunch?

I can't remember anything too horrific about working crunch, which might mark me out as somewhat lucky after five years' experience. A week or two of 12+ hour working days, maybe a dozen working Sundays and one time coming into the office at around four in the morning are about the worst I got.

If you could change one thing about the industry what would that be?

The over-reliance on crunch, which I feel is usually to the detriment of any project and I believe a key contributor to the high level of staff turnover in the industry.

Name:	Eamonn Mgherbi	**Currently working for:**	Avatar Games Recruitment
Age:	27	**Current role:**	Managing Director
Sex:	Male	**Length of Service:**	5 Years

Eamonn and I have been great friends since he helped me into my first Q.A. Manager role. A hard working dedicated recruitment agent, I've seen him leave his previous employer and set out to create his own recruitment agency. We started by looking at his career.

Why did you want to get into the games industry?

Ever since I could remember I had a controller in my hand. My first computer was a Commodore 64 and from then on I owned almost every other console that came out. The PlayStation was the console that made me think...wow I would love to be involved in the games industry. I spent a lot of my time researching various developers and the design process of many of the games made for the PS1. I also used to get involved with online mod groups for PC titles including, Delta Force 2, Quake, Counter Strike etc.

How long have you worked in the industry?

Just over 5 years professionally

Who have you worked for in the industry?

I previously worked for Amiqus then set up my own business in 2009 called Avatar.

What do you do in the industry?

I am a Recruiter working with a number of Developer and Publishers.

What would you say is the highlight of your career so far?

There have been quite a few in a short space of time, but taking Avatar to the develop awards in 2011 was a fantastic experience and a credit to the hard work of both myself and the team at Avatar.

How did you originally get into the industry and did you do anything unique to increase your chances?

A friend alerted me to a vacancy at Amiqus for an experienced recruiter with an interest in games. This felt like a dream switch from standard recruitment and gave me the opportunity to work in an industry that I'm truly passionate about.

How did you get into your current role?

I established Avatar with encouragement and support from friends within the industry. I wanted to offer a new approach to recruitment which was flexible and met the needs of both the clients and candidates by creating a blend of friendliness and professionalism.

What advice would you give to people looking to be a recruiter in the industry?

It takes a huge amount of drive, determination and sleepless nights. The hours can be pretty crazy as I need to remain flexible both for clients in the U.K. and across the globe. The job is incredibly rewarding, but due to the demanding, fast-paced nature of the industry it is not for the faint-hearted!

If hiring would you put more emphasis on education or experience?

Both are important, but I would say experience is key; this supported by passion and dedication will win you the role. I would recommend that graduates, who are interested in Level Design, put a show reel together which demonstrates their skills and previous projects and also for them to get involved in the mod communities as developers often keep a look for people who demonstrate great ideas.

Do you have any final thoughts for people hoping to become a recruiter in the games industry?

Self-belief and hard work in equal measures! Even when times get tough, work hard and continue to improve your performance...eventually you will get to the level you always wanted to achieve

With regards to actually working in the industry, what would you say is the best thing about your role?

I get to see all the games in development before they are released; it is always exciting to see what everyone is working on behind closed doors!

What's the worst thing about your role?

Long hours, although it is part of the job and I don't mind so much as I really love what I do.

So what's an average day for a recruiter like?

A strong cup of coffee first thing followed by a team chat then a quick check of emails from the night before, advert response etc. I would then call each person we send out to interview to make sure they are up to date with everything. Following that I would start to put a search plan in place for the particular project I'm working on and figure out who would be a good fit for the role.
It is the kind of job that gives you a new challenge everyday... just today I was busy preparing VAT returns, budgeting, meeting clients for lunch to review proposals for a recruitment plan they had...so a very busy and varied day!

So what are the longest hours you've worked during your busiest period?

My longest work day recorded was around 17 hours.

If you could change one thing about the industry what would that be?

I would say more financial incentives from the U.K. Government i.e. Tax Breaks.

How do you feel about the challenges women face in the industry?

It started as a very male dominated industry, but there are more and more women working in the industry now and I hope this continues to increase.

Do you think attitudes to women are changing in the industry?

I have noticed that more studios are looking for females to join their workforce which is a very positive thing and helps to promote diversity within our industry.

If you could offer one piece of advice to someone starting out in the industry what would that be?

Show ambition, determination and above all a passion for the games industry!

What sort of things should people starting out include on their C.V.'s?

If you are new to the industry then it's always handy to include anything that you are doing in your own time i.e. level design for mod groups or perhaps your own gaming art portfolio or programming demo code examples, also employers still want to see you were a good employee in your previous jobs so its key to include this although it may not seem relevant. List your achievements and the general skills you have acquired from those roles.

At what point should people think about contacting a games recruiter?

Recruiters are really useful in a number of different ways, they manage your interviews, they are usually first to hear about new jobs or jobs that perhaps aren't public, they can give you vital advice on your C.V. and general career advice so I would say you could use a recruiter at any point.

Do you enjoy working on the fringes of games development or would you rather be in the thick of it?

Personally I am happy doing what I do as I get to see what all studios are working on and have the chance to speak to new and interesting people every day. To be honest I think wherever you work in games there are fantastic opportunities to be explored as and we are lucky to work in the industry within any capacity.

As a recruiter do you only deal with development jobs or is it worth people getting in touch if they want to work in P.R. or a similar non-development role?

We deal with all areas of the games industry such as; H.R., Finance, Marketing & P.R., Distribution so it is definitely worth speaking with us.

Do you have any advice for people attempting to create their first show reel?

I think it is well worth speaking with people in the industry who are already in the profession or directly to companies/recruiters to see what to include; for example if you were trying to secure a job as an Animator then it's worth creating a show reel that shows as many scenarios as possible of movement i.e. a character carrying, pushing, facial expressions and even scenes that show how that person you have animated reacts when he is carrying heavy weight.

Some useful advice for us there, thanks for your time Eamonn.

Chapter 7: The secret level

In this section you'll find a range of useful bits, the glossary explains terms you may come across working in the industry. If you have any question please check out the F.A.Q.'s they might just contains the answer. Finally there are a range of helpful links and resources to help you find work, work experience, education and networking events.

Glossary:

A.I.

A.I. stands for artificial intelligence. Usually the computer controlled opponents in a videogame.

Attract mode

Attract mode is the rolling demo a videogame has. It usually begins and returns to the "Press start to play" screen. It covers some of the features of the game and is designed to attract people into buying the game, hence the name.

AAA game

A triple 'A' game is usually used to describe a very successful game, critically acclaimed and with high sales. Usually these calibre games may be used as an exclusive for a console manufacturer. Sometimes it is treated as a holy grail for game developers, it is what everyone hopes their product will become.

Alpha

Alpha is one of the key milestones. It is the second phase of development. See Chapter 1 for more info on milestones.

Asset

An asset is a thing in the game. It can be a type of object or a process/function within the title.

Assert

An assert is a method in the code of the game which will aid the coder in catching and fixing bugs.

Beta

Beta is the milestone directly after Alpha. A Beta build usually has most of content in, is working and is generally quite stable. See Chapter 1 for more info on milestones.

Beta Testing

Beta tests are becoming quite popular. A games company will release a unique limited version of the game to the public. This can be for used for two purposes, to allow the company to promote the title to the public and at the same time test the online servers prior to launch.

BGM

BGM is an abbreviation for background music.

Bug

A bug is a problem within the game this could range from graphics to sound, game play to A.I.

Build

When we create a version of the game, all the pieces come from the various teams. These are then built together to form the playable code, so a build is just a version of playable code.

Crunch

Crunch is a time frame around important milestones or towards the end of a project. When you're working during crunch you tend to do extended hours to meet deadlines.

Cut-scene

Cut-scenes cut away from the in-game action, usually to provide further story developments.

Debug

As the name suggests this is the process of removing bugs from the game.

Debug Tools

These are used to help Q.A. test the game. It could be a god mode, a level skipper or anything that will help Q.A. see and therefore test all parts of the game. Cheats are usually just debug tools left in the game upon release.

Dev. kit

A development kit is used by coders to aid development work on a console game. It is a special version of the console which you can attach to a P.C.

Development life cycle

The development life cycle is the process of taking a game idea and making it a real live product, for more information see Chapter 1.

Discography

A discography is a record of the games you have worked on, something you will work on over time in the industry and will form part of your resume.

EFIGS

EFIGS is a term used when localising a game, it stands for English, French, Italian, German and Spanish. These are the most common languages a video game is translated into.

FMV

Full motion video, this type of video is usually used in cut-scenes.

Focus Testing

Focus testing is when we get the target audience to try the game. This helps us establish if the game is good, fun and how it might be received.

Game Engine

The game engine is the code that handles all aspects of the game. How it processes physics, defines geometry and how it performs are all related to the game engine.

Game play mechanic

A game play mechanic is generally a rule within the game. How people have fun, control and work things out at different parts of the story are the mechanics of a game.

Gold

Gold is one of the key milestones. It is the final version of the game that all copies are made from. See Chapter 1 for more info on milestones.

HUD

The head up display is the information displayed to the user in a game. It could be lives, score, ammo, counts or laps. If the user needs to know something it forms part of the head up display.

I.P.

An I.P. is an internal product. You may have heard companies talking about a new or internal I.P. This just means a new title rather than a sequel.

Localisation

Localisation is when we translate the game to other languages. This usually includes text and voice.

LOT Check

LOT Check is Nintendo's submission process.

Modding

Modding a game means to modify it in some aspect. Often games are designed to allow a modding community to develop and add to the title as they wish. Previously some mods have led to a game in its own right.

N.D.A.

The non disclosure agreement is between you and the company. It is legally binding and states that you will not discuss the project or work you do.

N.P.C.

N.P.C. stands for non-player controlled character. This could be a quest giver, enemy or even a member of a crowd.

Placeholder

A placeholder is used in game development to reserve the space for something still in production. Creating a game can be quite memory intensive so a placeholder will reserve memory as well as locations for object, cut-scenes, artwork and audio.

Portfolio

A portfolio is much the same as a show reel (see below) it is used to demonstrate your skills and expertise and can take many forms.

Regression

Regression is when Q.A. checks a previously found bug to see if it still occurs is fixed or has caused a new problem to occur.

S.D.K.

Software development kits are the tools designers use to create the game. Some companies will even package a version of their S.D.K. to facilitate modding of a game.

SFX

SFX is the sound effects used within the game. These could be the sound of a heart beat when low on health or the sound a gun makes when reloading.

Shipped

This refers to the game being shipped to the shops and is often used in games development.

Show Reel

A show reel is a good idea. It's a demonstration of work you've done either while studying, in your free time or on previous projects. It's used during the recruitment phase and as such a well polished, unique show reel can make all the difference in your application.

Signed

When a project is signed, work can begin. The phrase comes from signing the contract with a publisher to begin work.

S.K.U.

S.K.U. is not actually specifically for video games. It is a number used to identify products in an inventory. Many catalogues and companies use S.K.U. (pronounced Skew) numbers, a good way to think of it is as individual retail discs.

Soak Test

A soak test is when the game is run for long periods of time to check for any problems which may occur with prolonged use.

Standards

Standards refer to the submission process or the standards required of a game by the console manufacturers prior to launch.

Submission

The process of submitting a game to a console manufacturer, for approval to sell the title on their hardware.

TCR

TCR is Sony's submission process.

Tech

This refers to the technologies studios create and employ to build a game. It could be anything from an advanced game engine to a realistic graphics engine or physics.

T.O.I.L.

Time off in lieu is not limited to the games industry. It just means for any extra time you work you get time off further down the line.

Tools

Developer tools are usually built in-house for the art or design team to utilise when creating the game they are designed and created to make the best use of games engines.

TRC

TRC is Microsoft's submission process.

U.I.

U.I. stands for user interface. All software products, not just games, need to consider the way information is presented to the user and how the user interacts with the product. This is the user interface. In video games a good example is the H.U.D. or control system.

U.S.P.

Unique selling points are the unique features of a game which making it appealing to the target audience.

Test Plan

We covered test plans in detail in the Q.A. chapter, but as the name suggests it's a plan covering the approach the Q.A. team will take to testing the game.

Test kit

A test kit is a special version of a console used for testing a game before release. It has certain features which aid in functional and submission testing.

Verification

Verification is another term used for the regression phase of a Q.A. test cycle.

Version

Each time the code is built into the game (all pieces put together) then that is known as a version of the game.

Version number

A version number is a unique number used to identify which build the version is. It is used for many different tracking purposes.

Vertical Slice

A vertical slice is normally used during the pitch phase of a project. It is a small bit of every part of the game. If you image a game's levels as layers of a cake, a slice of that cake is the vertical slice. The idea is to show off a small, but representative part of the overall game.

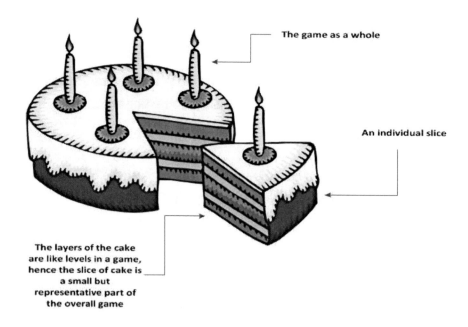

The game as a whole

An individual slice

The layers of the cake
are like levels in a game,
hence the slice of cake is
a small but
representative part of
the overall game

F.A.Q.s:

I only see jobs with X amount of experience, must have shipped a number of games. Does that mean there are no junior roles in my chosen dept?

A lot of junior roles are often filled internally (usually from Q.A.). If you're struggling to find any work in your chosen field, try Q.A. or other roles to gain some experience, advice and begin networking.

I'm a keen artist. Should I learn 3D Studio Max or Maya?

Each software package has its advantages and different studios use either of these products. So it would be ideal to learn at least the basics of both products to improve your employment chances.

Are there jobs out there? I'm struggling to find vacancies advertised.

Like any industry people are hired all the time. Try using the resource section to help expand your search or try considering further afield if you're still struggling as not every location has a development community.

If I get a qualification will I be at the standard required for any studio, large or small, for them to consider me for a job?

Different studios will use different tools and tech so there's no guarantee that your skill set will be a perfect match. This is another reason why your portfolio should be as good as possible. If you can prove your talents then any company will be willing to hire you and help you learn their own production processes.

What sort of work would a junior role initially contain?

This will vary greatly depending on the role. In essence just like any job it will be the more mundane work that you're likely to get while you gain experience. We all have to start off somewhere after all.

Are there studios that will be will to take on someone with just a diploma in games?

There are studios out there which will take people with no qualifications, so a diploma can only help.

Am I right in thinking a game designer is really just a visionary, the guy who comes up with ideas for games/concepts/storylines etc.? Who then just portrays his ideas to his team who would make the vision a reality?

No, that's really the director's role or the head of design. Really a designer tends to make other people's ideas actually work. This may be fleshing out a concept for game play or balancing the items within the title.

Does working on games stop you enjoying them in your free time?

This comes down to the individual. I still enjoy and love gaming, it's just I can see how it works. You very rarely get to work on games you'd actually buy so titles you want are still appealing and entertaining.

At the end of the interview what should I respond with if asked "Is there any questions you have for me?"... What would be a good response?

This is tricky. I would ask about crunch or whether they might be the chance of a permanent role if it's a temp contract. I would inquire as to how far in the development life cycle they are and when the title's due for release. These show that you're interested in the role and the overall nature of the title, but also that you would welcome the chance to stay on if it's a temporary role.

I've managed to get an internship at a games company. Can you offer any advice and is it possible to get a job from this?

It is possible to go from an internship or work experience programme into full time work. As you would expect these roles are highly sought after and the waiting lists can be quite long. It's absolutely worthwhile pursuing. I know many people who entered the industry in this way.

Should I wear a suit and tie to any interviews I get. I've been to one before and everyone was in T-shirts and jeans?

I always do. It's a sign that you take the job seriously and don't just see it as a fun place to work. Many people I know don't. It's really down to the individual and how they want to be seen.

Is there any advantage to gaining a job in games retail?

It's not going to give you an advantage, but it does help you to learn and investigate the market and consumer.

There seems to be a lot of roles you didn't cover, why is that?

There are just so many roles within the industry it would be impossible to cover every single one. I hope that I've given you a decent understanding about some of the roles out there.

Can I choose the games I work on?

Absolutely not! The projects you get assigned to are the ones you'll work on. It's highly unlikely to be your favourite game. A good developer will be able to be passionate about any project they find themselves on

I keep getting rejected what should I do?

The best advice I can offer is to up your game, raise the bar on the work you produce and make it the absolute best it can be. Add to your experience by applying to Beta tests, write to companies and see if they will review your work and don't forget getting online and asking your peers to critic it and don't give up!

I've been offered a role but it's not the role I wanted?

I'd suggest you take the role and get some experience and knowledge. You can always keep looking for the ideal role as you work.

People say I should network, can you give me any advice how I can do this?

This is a tricky one. I'd advise checking out games conferences and other similar events. There are also many online forums and websites worth checking out. For more info. see the networking resources section.

I'm desperate to work in games but I haven't any experience yet. Should I still contact industry recruitment agencies?

Recruitment agencies will get junior roles from time to time so it's worth getting in touch just in case.

Resources

Please note all URL's are correct at the time of writing.

Events:

- The Eurogamer Expo is fast becoming the U.K.'s top gaming event. Not only can you play the latest games, but there's also a career fair and many discussion panels to sink your teeth into. More info. can be found at http://www.eurogamer.net/expo/
- "Women in Games" champions women in the industry. A great networking event with many speakers, more info. can be found on their website: http://www.womeningames.com/
- The Develop Conference is one of the oldest and most respected U.K. games industry events. Each year we descend on Brighton for a weekend of networking, discussions and events check out http://www.developconference.com/ for more info.
- For information on the many other events around the world each year, check out the events page at Gi.biz. This handy calendar covers almost every event around the world. http://www.gamesindustry.biz/network/events

Networking:

- LinkedIn has fast become the business social networking site. Many games companies and their staff can be found on this site: http://www.linkedin.com/
- Names in Games are a social networking site just like LinkedIn. It is however exclusive for the games industry: http://www.namesingames.com/
- http://www.Gamesindustry.biz is the place to get all of your industry news, with so many industry professionals on the site daily you can easily make new contacts on the site.

Studios:

- http://www.gamedevmap.com/ This handy websites shows you almost all of the studios around the world, as well as publishers and organisations. This really is the website you need when looking for potential employers.

Recruitment Agencies:

- Avatar Games: http://avatar-games.co. uk/
- OPM: http://www.opmjobs.com
- Aardvark swift: http://www.aswift.com/
- Datascope: http://www.datascope.co.uk/
- Amiqus Games: http://www.amiqus.com/
- Interactive selection: http://www.interactiveselection.com/index.asp
- Semag: http://semag.co.uk/

Job sites:

- Http://www.Gamesindustry.biz
- http://www.Gamesrecruit.co.uk
- http://www.gamesjobsdirect.com/
- http://www.mcvuk.com/
- http://jobs.next-gen.biz/

Education:

- http://www.train2game.com
- http://www.ucas.com/